LOUISVILLE

A River Serenade

L O U I S

By Bob Hill & Dan Dry

Art Direction by Brian Groppe

Profiles by WordWeavers, Inc.

T O W E R Y   P U B L I S H I N G ,   I N C .

VILLE

A River Serenade

Sponsored by the Louisville Area Chamber of Commerce and the Greater Louisville Economic Development Partnership

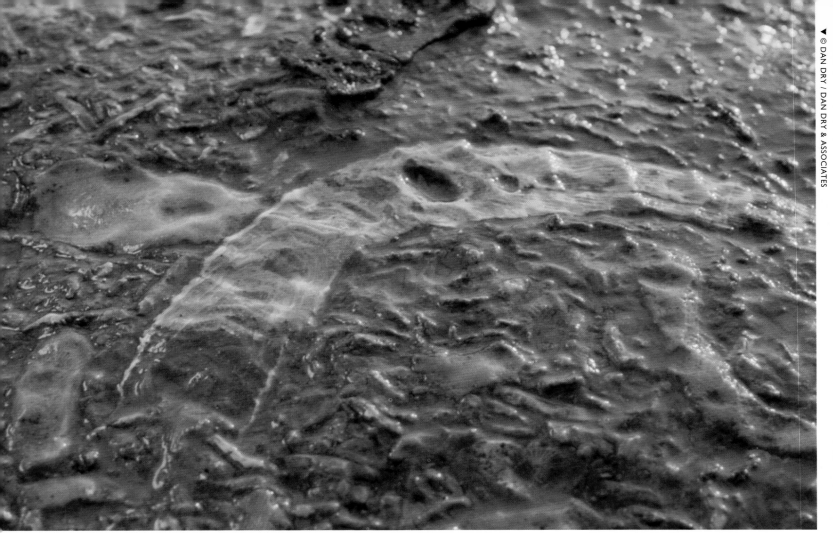

MORNING ON THE OHIO. GLOWING
IN THE EARLY SUNLIGHT, THE
HISTORIC PADDLE WHEELER *BELLE
OF LOUISVILLE*, A REMINDER OF THE
THRIVING RIVERBOAT DAYS OF
YESTERYEAR, AWAITS ANOTHER
EXCURSION (PAGES 2 AND 3).

LIBRARY OF CONGRESS CATALOGING-IN-PUBLICATION DATA

Hill, Bob, 1942-

    Louisville : a river serenade / by Bob Hill ; corporate profiles
by WordWeavers, Inc. ; art direction by Brian Groppe.

       p.   cm. — (Urban tapestry series)

    "Sponsored by the Louisville Area Chamber of Commerce and the
Greater Louisville Economic Development Partnership."

    Includes index.

    ISBN 1-881096-26-2

    1. Louisville (Ky.)—Pictorial works.   I. WordWeavers, Inc.
II. Groppe, Brian.   III. Title.   IV. Series.

F459.L843H55   1995

976.9'44—dc20   95-51557
                                                           CIP

Towery Publishing, Inc., 1835 Union Avenue, Memphis, TN 38104

PUBLISHER: J. Robert Towery
EXECUTIVE PUBLISHER: Jenny McDowell
NATIONAL SALES MANAGER: Stephen Hung
NATIONAL MARKETING DIRECTOR: Eleanor D. Carey
PROJECT DIRECTORS: Judy Blankenbaker, John Lorenzo, Harry Nelson
EXECUTIVE EDITOR: David Dawson
SENIOR EDITOR: Michael C. James
PROFILES MANAGER / ASSOCIATE EDITOR: Lynn Conlee
ASSOCIATE EDITORS: Mary Jane Adams, Lori Bond, Carlisle Hacker, Jason Vest
EDITORIAL INTERN: Kristen Taylor
EDITORIAL CONTRIBUTORS: David Hoefer, Lee Dunham, Mark Besten, Robin Morgan, Ninette Shorter
PROFILE DESIGNER: Laurie Lewis
TECHNICAL DIRECTOR: William H. Towery
PRODUCTION MANAGER: Brenda Pattat

URBAN
TAPESTRY
SERIES
TOWERY
PUBLISHING, INC.

A treasure trove for paleontologists, the fossil beds at the Falls of the Ohio River (opposite) provide an educational opportunity for visitors to the Indiana side of the river. At the same time, visitors can also view a more modern sight, Louisville's panoramic skyline (above).

The soaring skyscrapers of Louisville's downtown are framed by the trees of the southern Indiana shore (pages 6 and 7).

BY BOB HILL

*A*LMOST ANY DAY OF THE YEAR, you can find someone standing on the Ohio River overlook in downtown Louisville, staring off into the distance, caught up in the power and timelessness of the river. ◆ At special

THE LUMINESCENCE OF LOUISVILLE'S NIGHTLIFE TINTS THE EVENING SKY (LEFT). THE SUN LAYS A CARPET OF GOLD ON THE OHIO RIVER AS PLEASURE BOATS TAKE THEIR FINAL TURN ON THE WATER (OPPOSITE).

moments, as the sun slips behind the nearby Indiana hills, casting rosy pink flares on dark water, the charm is solitary and personal. Other evenings, say in mid-April, when the waterfront erupts in a boiling fury of pre-Kentucky Derby fireworks—affectionately known as Thunder Over Louisville—a visitor might be joined by 400,000 close friends. Louisville is very good at tossing a giant party.

The Kentucky Derby Festival—with its Great Balloon Race, Great Steamboat Race, and Great Burgoo—lasts almost two weeks before the horses and hyperbole are shipped out of town. The truth is, the city is a lot more comfortable with itself—and its many visitors—the other 50 weeks of the year.

Louisvillians—and the nearby residents of southern Indiana—talk easily of their quality of life, the way honey slides from a pitcher. They are justifiably secure in it, practically smug about it; the reasons are as varied as basketball and ballet, as compatible as

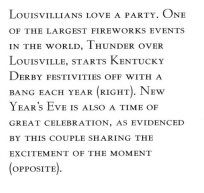

LOUISVILLIANS LOVE A PARTY. ONE OF THE LARGEST FIREWORKS EVENTS IN THE WORLD, THUNDER OVER LOUISVILLE, STARTS KENTUCKY DERBY FESTIVITIES OFF WITH A BANG EACH YEAR (RIGHT). NEW YEAR'S EVE IS ALSO A TIME OF GREAT CELEBRATION, AS EVIDENCED BY THIS COUPLE SHARING THE EXCITEMENT OF THE MOMENT (OPPOSITE).

the city's park benches and ever-lengthening RiverWalk that wanders the river's edge for miles. It's an attitude that's received a lot of outside affirmation: Three years in a row, *Places Rated Almanac* has ranked Louisville as one of America's 10 best places to live.

Louisville has its share of urban problems, but they seem more manageable, more open to solutions, with dozens of organizations willing to try. Nothing sums up its giving spirit more than the annual WHAS Crusade for Children, a yearlong campaign that is spearheaded by 10,000 volunteer firemen and that brings in more than $4 million for needy children.

City salesmen have their requisite slogan, "Louisville: A World-Class City," but it's a boast that goes much more to the heart than to the head. The city's expanding airport was recently renamed Louisville International Airport, while cynics cheerfully noted that the only direct international flights out of town were those flown by UPS, the city's largest employer.

The truth is, Louisville has always been hard to define, difficult to label with preciseness. Because its name carries so much historical baggage, visitors are always surprised to learn that its population is only about 270,000, although the metro area nudges just past 1 million strong. The guests must like the city's ambience; although about 50th in size, it always ranks in the top 25 cities in the nation in tourist business and fourth in available exhibit space.

Louisville's personality has been shaped by state history; Kentucky's brawling and often counterproductive state politics; its border-city status during the Civil War; and its neither

Honoring one of the nation's apostles of liberty, a statue of Thomas Jefferson stands tall in front of the Jefferson County Courthouse (left). Mirrored by a modern office tower, Louisville's Cathedral of the Assumption—one of the oldest churches in the nation—is undergoing major renovation to preserve its architectural splendor (opposite).

southern-fish nor northern-fowl location on the Kentucky-Indiana border. Cartographers will gleefully note—for whatever it's worth—that Louisville is actually closer to Canada than it is to Memphis, Tennessee. Still, the city's professional hockey team has been dubbed—with a decidedly American touch—the River Frogs.

In a biographical nutshell, Louisville is an almost midwestern city that has southern pretensions and civilities and that was a staging area for Union troops from its Indiana border. The civility came honestly; in its early life, Kentucky was a far-flung county of Virginia. Nor can you ignore Louisville's current eastern pretensions; many of its citizens enjoy flitting off to New York on long weekends for some East Coast culture. ▶

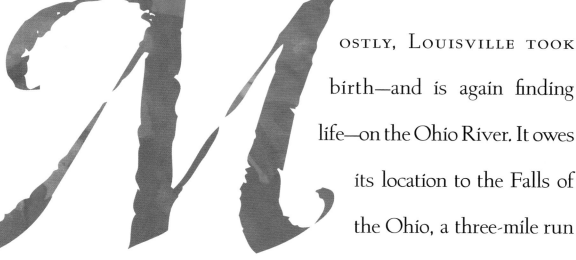

OSTLY, LOUISVILLE TOOK birth—and is again finding life—on the Ohio River. It owes its location to the Falls of the Ohio, a three-mile run of exposed rock and tumbling rapids, the only

KENNETH HAYDEN

FOSSIL HUNTERS EXPLORE THE ROCKY RECORD OF THE DEVONIAN PERIOD AT THE FALLS OF THE OHIO RIVER (LEFT). HOME OF LOUISVILLE'S FOUNDER, GEORGE ROGERS CLARK, HISTORIC LOCUST GROVE IS OPEN FOR TOURS AND SPECIAL EVENTS (OPPOSITE).

natural impediment in the entire, 981-mile course of the Ohio River. ◆ Those rapids forced George Rogers Clark, one of history's forgotten heroes, to lead his band of 150 soldiers and 80 settlers to a small island just off the Kentucky shoreline in 1778. Clark and his tough, raggedy frontiersmen-soldiers went on to seize the entire Northwest Territory from the British, helping expand the country by a half-dozen states.

Two years later Clark's little settlement moved ashore to Kentucky and became Louisville, named in honor of King Louis XVI. A grand statue of Clark pointing north by northwest now graces the downtown overlook. Local Hoosiers like to think he is pointing fondly toward Indiana.

Louisville grew swiftly; it had to. River traffic was forced to stop at its shore, at least until a fine canal with locks and a dam was built around the Falls of the Ohio. By 1850 Louisville was one of the 10 largest cities in the country, along with other cities

A STAUNCH SUPPORTER OF THE AMERICAN REVOLUTION, FRANCE'S KING LOUIS XVI INSPIRED THE NAME OF THE RIVER SETTLEMENT THAT BECAME LOUISVILLE (RIGHT). A LIFE-SIZE PORTRAIT OF MADAME ADELAIDE, AUNT OF LOUIS XVI, COMMANDS THE ATTENTION OF VISITORS TO THE J.B. SPEED ART MUSEUM (OPPOSITE).

© DAN DRY / DAN DRY & ASSOCIATES

of great romance and promise in the nation's sprawling interior: Cincinnati, St. Louis, and Chicago.

The river supplied Louisville with its lifeblood, the stream of men and women who arrived at its muddy waterfront by steamboat and flatboat—or as slaves. They stayed to become its future: laborers, accountants, policemen, educators, politicians, gamblers, housemaids, merchants, and manufacturers.

In 1884 one of these entrepreneurs, a young woodworker named Bud Hillerich, agreed to turn a baseball bat on a lathe as a favor to a local baseball player. Thus was born the Louisville Slugger, the greatest icon in the history of the sport, an icon now being honored with a 120-foot, 80,000-pound steel replica at the new Hillerich & Bradsby Co. plant and museum on Main Street, just one block off the river.

MADAME ADELAIDE DE FRANCE
fille de Louis XV
Peinte par Mme Adélaïde LABILLE-GUIARD en 1787

The newcomers settled in distinct neighborhoods and built distinctive businesses and homes, which are still a marvelous feature of the city. German immigrants, who settled in Butchertown, drove great herds of muddy, squealing livestock down its streets to the Bourbon stockyards, the oldest stockyard in continuing operation in the country. They soon lived in one-story "shotgun homes," houses 20 feet wide and 80 feet deep, so named because you could supposedly fire a shotgun through the front door and have the buckshot rush out the back door without sustaining any damage.

Irish Hill, an area of high ground near downtown Louisville,

▲ LYNN SHEA

was home to slaughterhouses, as well as the largest whiskey warehouse in the world. Other Irish immigrants settled in Limerick, an area just south of downtown where farm fields were quickly converted into modest, wood-framed homes.

The very wealthy lived and played in Old Louisville, Victorian enclaves on tree-lined streets south of downtown. Most of those old homes are now divided into apartments, many currently occupied by young professionals.

The names of the neighborhoods in and around Louisville are lyrical and evocative. Anchorage, a charming community of large houses and wide yards, was named by a retired riverboat captain who planted an old anchor in his front yard, declaring the place his final anchorage. Lake Dreamland was first a resort, then more of a nightmare as its inadequate cottages crumbled. The early African-American families settled in neighborhoods such as Berrytown and Griffytown, building them into lasting communities.

TODAY, OLD LOUISVILLE IS UNDERGOING A REBIRTH AS YOUNG PROFESSIONALS HAVE DISCOVERED THE CHARM OF ITS STATELY MANSIONS (LEFT). A SWEEPING STAIRCASE INVITES PASSERSBY INTO ONE OF THE MANY ELEGANT VICTORIAN HOMES IN THE OLD LOUISVILLE NEIGHBORHOOD (OPPOSITE).

A freed slave began Petersburg in a vast, swampy area known as Wet Woods, and later known as Newburg.

Louisville celebrates its rich cultural and ethnic history endlessly—its Irish folk with an Irish Family Fest at Bellarmine College; its Germans with a downtown party in August, when polka music and grape-stomping events spill over onto the riverfront Belvedere. If that's not enough, the Louisville Jaycees sponsor an Oktoberfest each fall.

The African-American community—now about 30 percent of the city's population—proudly celebrates its heritage and its many educators, artisans, and entertainers at events throughout

BAGPIPERS REGALE ONLOOKERS AT CITYFAIR, A CELEBRATION OF THE ETHNIC DIVERSITY OF LOUISVILLE'S RESIDENTS (RIGHT). THE BELOVED COOKIE LADY, ONE OF LOUISVILLE'S BEST-KNOWN ENTREPRENEURS, BLENDS THE TASTES OF AFRICA AND THE UNITED STATES WITH HER POPULAR HOME-BAKED TREATS (OPPOSITE).

the year. During Derby Week, this community in particular celebrates the prowess of the African-American jockeys who won the early Kentucky Derbys.

Many events—the CityFair in downtown Louisville is the best example—bring everyone together near the river for a pulsating mix of music, fun, and food.

Louisvillians love their 8,600 acres of parks, which spread across the city like green jewels on an urban necklace, each connected by long, tree-lined parkways. The largest were designed by Frederick Law Olmsted, the man who designed New York's Central Park. Each Louisville park is named for a Native American tribe. When Olmsted laid out the system a century ago, many of his parks were so far out of town that local residents thought his reach had far exceeded the city's grasp. As Louisville grew, eventually surrounding his parklands, Olmsted's foresight was universally praised.

Take a tour of Olmsted's parks on a summer night; listen to the music of the city and its people. Chickasaw and Shawnee parks, at the city's western shoulder, brush up against the Ohio River. Their broad, green expanses lap up against some of the city's finest older homes. Drive the park roads on any weekend, and you'll find cars parked under monstrous oak and maple trees, the air filled with the sounds of family picnics, rap music, and the steady beat of basketballs on cement and asphalt courts.

Iroquois Park, at the southern edge of the city, has a fine over-look showing downtown Louisville from the back side, revealing its developing skyline and its sense of place on the river.

BLESSED WITH ONE OF THE FINEST PARK SYSTEMS IN THE UNITED STATES, LOUISVILLIANS ARE NEVER MORE THAN A SHORT DRIVE AWAY FROM PASTORAL RETREATS.

Almost all the parks have golf courses, tennis courts, basket-ball courts, softball fields, and walking and jogging trails. None of these amenities are more popular than those at Seneca and Cherokee parks in the Highlands, an area so named because it was safe from the occasionally rampaging Ohio River. Veteran Louisvillians—and an amazingly large number of people born in Louisville never leave—still recall their floods almost fondly, the 1937 inundation still being excellent fodder for nostalgia. ▶

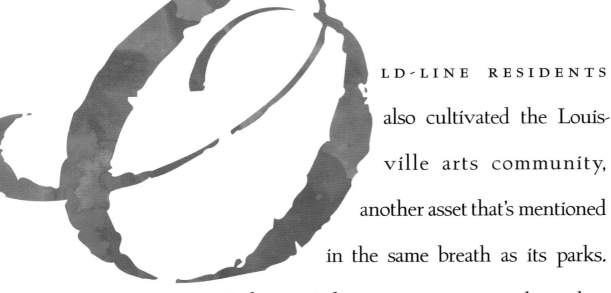

LD-LINE RESIDENTS also cultivated the Louisville arts community, another asset that's mentioned in the same breath as its parks. Perhaps it's because so many working-class

From homespun crafts to internationally recognized arts organizations, Louisville offers a rainbow of cultural colors. Resplendent costumes are a staple of the Kentucky Opera Association (right). A skilled crafts woman pieces together one of many sought-after Kentucky quilts (opposite).

Louisvillians came from rural Kentucky. Maybe it's due to the city's southern, partly aristocratic flavor. Whatever the reasons, Louisville has a tremendously popular and diverse arts community: orchestra, ballet, opera, local theater, Broadway shows, bluegrass, rock, jazz, zydeco, blues, pop, and—of course—country.

Granted, it may take a while for the big Broadway shows to travel the 900 miles inland to Louisville, but the ticket prices will be more reasonable, and you can park within four blocks of the theater.

The performing venues are as diverse as the music. The Kentucky Center for the Arts is a gleaming success story, its mirrored front reflecting the cast-iron storefronts of another city treasure, Main Street. The center has two main stages and an experimental theater upstairs, showcasing such greats as *Phantom of the Opera.*

The newly renovated Actors Theatre of Louisville offers some of the best, most innovative regional theater in the country. The Palace Theatre, an old downtown movie house returned to its

OUTDOOR CONCERTS ARE A SIGNA-TURE SUMMER SPECIALTY OF THE LOUISVILLE ORCHESTRA (RIGHT). EQUALLY WELL KNOWN AMONG LOCALS, THESE PLAYFUL SCULPTURES BY JEAN DUBUFFET GREET PATRONS OF THE KENTUCKY CENTER FOR THE ARTS (OPPOSITE).

◀ © DAN DRY / DAN DRY & ASSOCIATES

baroque glory, brings back many of the golden oldie set. The $2.3 million Louisville Ballet Center is taking shape. The accommodating Freedom Hall at the Kentucky State Fairgrounds can hold almost 20,000 screaming fans who risk perpetual deafness as rock—and country—groups move through, amplifiers blazing.

Drive along Bardstown Road on a Friday night, and you can taste the city's flavor in any one of a dozen nightspots, mostly smaller clubs where hopeful blues, rock, and pop musicians—not to mention poets—live together in dim and distant corners.

Blue-collar or tux-and-tails, the Louisville culture is underlined with a love of basketball. The absolute best way to start an argument in any nightspot is to declare undying devotion to either the University of Louisville, with its two NCAA basketball championships, or its bitter rival, the University of Kentucky,

which has five championship banners hanging from its rafters and a lot of fans living on Louisville soil. A recurring problem in divorce cases involving fans of either school is who gets the season tickets.

In the off-season, at least, basketball fans can calm down at the booming Louisville Zoo, which always has some exotic animal on display, or the Speed Art Museum, also set to expand. Or they can visit Kentucky Kingdom-The Thrill Park, which, as Louisville's largest tourist attraction, captured more than 1 million visitors in 1993. Hot dogs never taste better than at Cardinal Stadium, where the Class AAA Louisville Redbirds were the first minor-league team to draw 1 million fans. If there's one complaint about all the

KINGS OF THE DIAMOND, THE 1995 AMERICAN ASSOCIATION CHAMPION LOUISVILLE REDBIRDS ARE ONE OF THE MOST POPULAR CLASS AAA BASEBALL CLUBS IN HISTORY (LEFT).

THE "MANE EVENT" AMONG THE RESIDENTS OF THE LOUISVILLE ZOO, THESE LIONS ENJOY A NATURALIZED SETTING (OPPOSITE).

Louisville entertainment, it's that there's always more going on than there is time—or local money—to support fully. Louisville hasn't turned out a lot of local sports heroes, but when it has, they've turned out to be good ones—baseball's Pee Wee Reese, football's Paul Horning, basketball's Denny Crum, and auto racing's Danny Sullivan. Horning and Reese played high school ball in Louisville, Horning going on to Notre Dame and Reese climbing utility poles as a line splicer before deciding there had to be a better way to make a living. Reese never forgot Louisville, making it home in the off-season, but his success in baseball surprised him. "I'm four years off a utility pole in Louisville," Reese once said about his first game in the World Series. "I'm in Yankee Stadium. I look around and say, 'What the hell am I doing here?'"

Louisvillians also find great pride in other native sons and daughters of a more belletristic mode: Hollywood's Tom Cruise and Irene Dunne, gonzo writer Hunter S. Thompson, Pulitzer Prize-winning playwright Marsha Norman, Supreme Court Justice Louis Brandeis, journalist Diane Sawyer, and jazzman Lionel Hampton, who gives everyone good vibes.

For all their fame, no one can compare to Muhammad Ali, the "Louisville Lip," who left his hometown to become one of the most famous people in the world. In his heyday, Ali loved to come back to Louisville and walk its streets; he was a parade just waiting to happen. Small children would walk up to him for a hug; adults followed him just to watch the show. Ali would playfully keep them at bay, tossing soft punches, bobbing and

LOCAL BOXING LEGEND MUHAMMAD ALI'S NAME—AMONG THE GREATEST IN THE HISTORY OF SPORTS—FLOATS LIKE A BUTTERFLY OVER THE DOWNTOWN THOROUGHFARE RECHRISTENED IN HIS HONOR (RIGHT). THE LOUISVILLE SLUGGER, WEAPON OF CHOICE FOR BASEBALL'S GREATEST HITTERS, RECENTLY MOVED PRODUCTION BACK TO THE CITY OF ITS ORIGIN (OPPOSITE).

weaving, or breaking into the Ali shuffle.

"I AM THE GREATEST," he would proclaim, his face a mask of mock anger. Then Ali would sit for hours signing autographs and talking of his religion, Islam, as long lines would form across a building lobby and even into the street. A long overdue Muhammad Ali museum has now been opened in the downtown Galleria, just a short distance from Muhammad Ali Boulevard, which stretches all the way across town. "There's only one fighter who's a thoroughbred and a native son," Mayor Jerry Abramson said at the museum's dedication, as Ali sat near him. "Muhammad Ali is number one forever."

Like Ali, Louisville is now finding joy in returning to its roots. Hurt by a loss of manufacturing jobs in the 1970s, it has recovered with the growth of UPS, two huge Ford Motor Company plants, the steady presence of General Electric, and the city's

rising fame as a medical and health insurance center. Along with that growth came the redevelopment of Louisville's waterfront—an awakening mirrored by the parklike development of the southern Indiana riverfront and the addition of the magnificent Falls of the Ohio Museum.

It hasn't been easy. Progress has not been steady; at times it seemed you could build a new bridge across the river just by stacking on top of one another the various expensive studies of where to build what. If anything, Louisville and its leaders have often been a little too patient about change. But a challenge issued by Frederick Law Olmsted a century ago eventually took hold:

A SCENIC MIX OF NATURAL AND MAN-MADE BEAUTY DELIGHTS LOUISVILLE VISITORS AND RESIDENTS YEAR-ROUND, BUT MANY ENJOY THE MULTIHUED PALETTE OF AUTUMN MOST OF ALL.

". . . if you want the city to have broad and tranquil meadow spaces, with shadows of great spreading trees slanting across them, and areas of turf for lawn games, that park would be by the Ohio."

That park is now a little more homemade than Olmsted may have envisioned—more than $200 million has been spent or committed in various waterfront projects—but its early phases have been completed, and the grass seed has already gone to work.

Waterfront planners couldn't resist capitalizing the name of every proposed feature: the Great Lawn, the Upland Meadow, Linear Park, the Plaza, Waterfront Park, Pilots Harbor. When finished (it already connects to the Belvedere and the RiverWalk), the park will offer acres, even miles, of riverfront enjoyment.

Already in place is the Falls Fountain, a gift to the city by its prominent Bingham family. The fountain fires a fleur-de-lis spray— the city trademark—a hundred feet into the air. The cascading water, bathed in bright light, lands not far from the place where George Rogers Clark first set foot 200 years ago.

Plying the waters near the fountain is the *Belle of Louisville*, an old paddle wheeler on which Louisvillians lavish constant and sturdy affection, if not love. On summer nights (special moments indeed), with the Belle's calliope in full musical cry, the steam from its engines billowing above the flashing paddle wheel, it's yet another reminder that there's no better place to find romance on the river. ■

WHEN ALL IS SAID AND DONE, THE OHIO RIVER IS STILL AT THE HEART OF LOUISVILLE LIFE. THE *BELLE OF LOUISVILLE* CHURNS UPSTREAM UNDER A SNOWY PLUME OF STEAM (RIGHT). THE CROWN JEWEL OF LOUISVILLE'S WATERFRONT, THE FALLS FOUNTAIN CELEBRATES THE MAJESTY OF THE RIVER (OPPOSITE).

◀ JOHN NATION

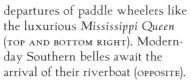

*L*OUISVILLE CONTINUES TO CELE-brate the pageantry of its river history. The calliope (ABOVE) is the traditional instrument that announces the arrivals and departures of paddle wheelers like the luxurious *Mississippi Queen* (TOP AND BOTTOM RIGHT). Modern-day Southern belles await the arrival of their riverboat (OPPOSITE).

The streets of Louisville are frequently awash with the sights and sounds of festivals and fairs. The annual CityFair brings carnival rides to the downtown business district (RIGHT).

Young Louisvillians enjoy the classic fun of the Ferris wheel (OPPOSITE).

𝒜 LONGTIME CENTER OF MANU-
facturing, Louisville has maintain-
ed an industrial base even while
its service sector has grown.
The industrial conveyor system
(PAGE 40) is reflected in cultural
structures such as the Kentucky
Center for the Arts (PAGE 41).
PAGE 40: JEANNE FREIBERT
PAGE 41: RALPH H. SIDWAY

*T*HE ACTIVE INTEREST OF BUSINESS leaders—such as David Jones (ABOVE) and the late Wendell Cherry, cofounders of Humana Inc.—has infused Louisville's urban landscape with distinctive shapes that include the sculpture on the riverfront Belvedere (TOP RIGHT) and the Humana Building (BOTTOM RIGHT), which is recognized as a major achievement of American architecture.

*L*IKE MANY AMERICAN CITIES, the vitality of Louisville's downtown retail center has waned, thanks in part to the city's spread to the suburbs. In recent years, though, downtown shopping has been rejuvenated by the Louisville Galleria, a glass-enclosed mall, and the colorful Toonerville II's, named for the golden-age comic strip.

*T*HE SETTING SUN BURNISHES
the glass, steel, and marble sur-
faces of Louisville's commercial
profile (PRECEDING PAGES).

PAGES 44 AND 45: JOHN NATION

*W*HILE KNOWN FOR ITS DOWNHOME charm, Louisville has its high-rise sophistication, too, from spacious offices (OPPOSITE) to luxurious penthouse apartments (ABOVE).

*T*HE CLASSICAL LINES OF GREEK Revival architecture (RIGHT) segue into the clean, postmodern design of the new Providian Center (OPPOSITE), reinforcing Louisville's reputation for notable architecture.

𝒜s Louisville grew and prospered in the late 19th and early 20th centuries, public monuments were built on a grand scale, and with strict attention to detail (above). Examples include a gargoyle on the Louisville Free Public Library (opposite, left), and the stained glass fleur-de-lis, symbolizing Louisville's cultural link to France (opposite, right).

𝒯HE INTERPLAY OF LIGHT AND
shadow illuminates Louisville's
skyways and bridges.

The Louisville Water Company's Crescent Hill reservoir was an engineering marvel of its day. The sculptural quality of its elaborate metalworks lends refinement to this Gothic Revival landmark (PAGES 54-56).

PAGES 54 AND 55: KENNETH HAYDEN

*A*RCHITECTURAL STRUCTURES in Louisville are often works of art. Some focus on ornate details (TOP) to attract attention, while others provide a commanding view away from the building. For example, the skyway connecting the Galt House hotel complex frames the view from the riverfront toward bustling Main Street (BOTTOM).

$\mathcal{A}$ STRONG MANUFACTURING BASE continues to drive Louisville's economy. The city has attracted many new industries, while successfully encouraging established firms to modernize.

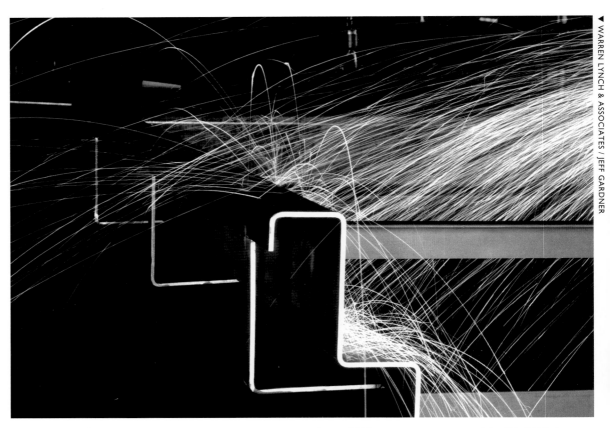

JEFFBOAT

AMERICA'S LARGEST INLAND SHIPBUILDER.

𝒟ISTILLED BEVERAGES HAVE BEEN an economic mainstay of Louisville and the surrounding area for years. Brown-Forman Corporation's rooftop proudly displays one of Kentucky's most famous products, bourbon whiskey (TOP LEFT). Louisville's once-proud beer-making industry is being reborn, thanks to new local microbreweries (BOTTOM LEFT).

On the Indiana side of the river, JeffBoat (TOP RIGHT), a leading shipbuilder, traces its history back to the steamboat days, which are highlighted at the Howard Steamboat Museum, just down the street in Jeffersonville (BOTTOM RIGHT).

*R*USTING TRAIN WHEELS RECALL the romance of the rails. Even today, Louisville is a major railroad shipping center.

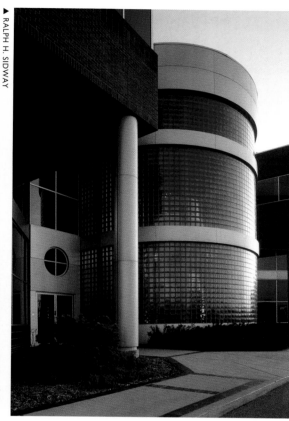

*E*FFICIENT AIR TRAVEL HAS ALWAYS been foremost in Louisville. Bowman Field, the city's first airport, was the busiest in the nation during World War II. Its Art Deco structure is a historic landmark (TOP LEFT).

At the recently expanded Louisville International Airport (TOP RIGHT AND BOTTOM), travelers enjoy convenient service to most major cities, without the accompanying congestion.

*L*OUISVILLE IS A CITY HAUNTED by beauty. A ghostly fog embraces the riverfront (ABOVE), while steam rises around the paddle wheels of the *Belle of Louisville* (OPPOSITE).

*E*NCHANTED EVENINGS IN Louisville: Horse-drawn carriages and brightly lit facades distinguish nightlife in the city.

the old spaghetti factory

LOUISVILLE OFFERS A WIDE ARRAY of cultural diversions, including music, theater, and opera, as well as the J.B. Speed Art Museum (RIGHT) and Louisville Ballet (OPPOSITE, BOTTOM).

*B*LUES HAVE A PROMINENT PLACE on the menu at the African-American Music Festival.

*T*HEATER IN LOUISVILLE ISN'T JUST for adults. Stage One (TOP LEFT AND BOTTOM RIGHT) and Walden Theater (BOTTOM LEFT) are noted for the high quality of their children's productions.

𝓑RINGING THE PAST INTO THE future: Louisvillians enjoy finding new and creative uses for old buildings. The handsome facade of the Ohio Theater distinguishes Theater Square in the heart of downtown (PAGE 72). The old Louisville Normal School is now home to renowned Joe Ley Antiques (PAGE 73).

PAGE 72: CHARLENE FARIS / HILLSTROM STOCK
PAGE 73: WILLIAM N. CLARK

$\mathcal{I}$N LOUISVILLE, SPRING MEANS Kentucky Derby festivities. The Pegasus Parade (PAGES 74 AND 75) gives Louisville businesses a chance to trumpet their civic pride.

A CONSUMABLE FEAST: FROM watermelon to burgoo, Louisville is famous for its inventive cuisine.

*L*OCAL RESTAURATEURS LYNN Winters (BOTTOM LEFT) and Kathy Carey (TOP RIGHT) have earned national recognition for their culinary expertise.

*A*NNUAL FESTIVALS, LIKE THE St. James Art Fair and American Music Festival, highlight the artistry and craftsmanship of the Louisville area and bring the community together in celebration.

A R I V E R S E R E N A D E

𝒯HE STRAINS OF BEAUTIFUL MUSIC can be heard around the city of Louisville. Students learn their craft at the University of Louisville School of Music.

*M*USICIANS AT THE GOSPEL Shout Out raise their voices to God in joyful song.

WARREN LYNCH & ASSOCIATES / JEFF GARDNER

*I*MMIGRANT GROUPS SETTLING IN the area brought with them deeply held religious beliefs that are reflected in Louisville's many places of worship, including St. Joseph's (RIGHT AND OPPOSITE, BOTTOM LEFT), the Cathedral of the Assumption (OPPOSITE, BOTTOM RIGHT), and St. Michael Orthodox Church (OPPOSITE, TOP).

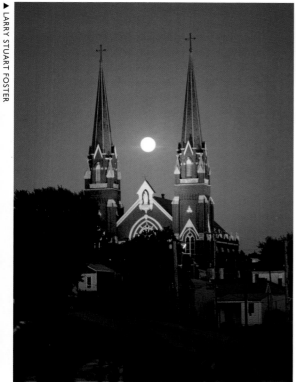

*F*OLK ART AND RELIGION COMBINE
in a tapestry of the spirit.

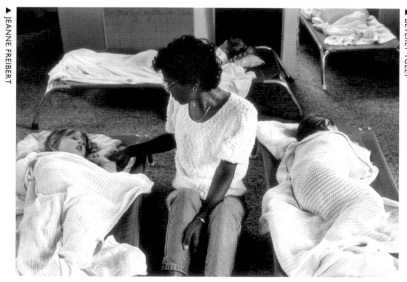

*L*OUISVILLE, CITY WITH A HEART, reaches out to those in need. Nationwide recognition has come to its many ministries and community services.

*L*ONG REGARDED AS A CENTER OF health care innovation, Louisville is home to many of the nation's most prestigious medical providers.

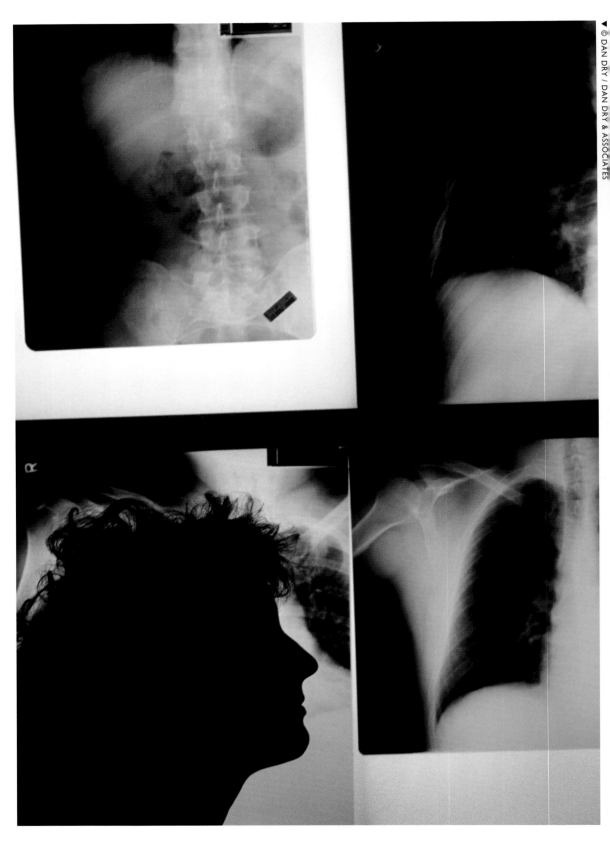

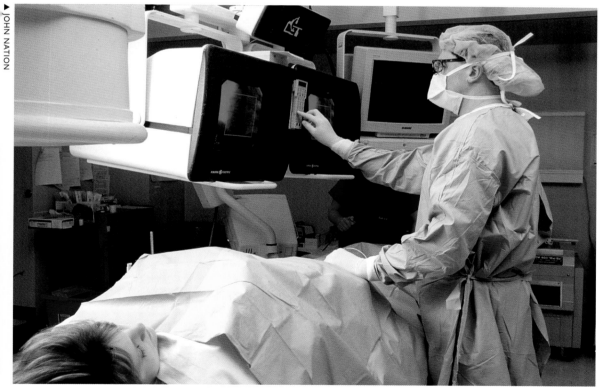

*I*N A CASE OF LIFE REFLECTING ART, the city is full of the inhabitants of the imagination: artists.

*F*ROM ELEMENTARY SCHOOL TO postgraduate education, Louisville is preparing citizens of all ages for the dynamic economy of the 21st century.

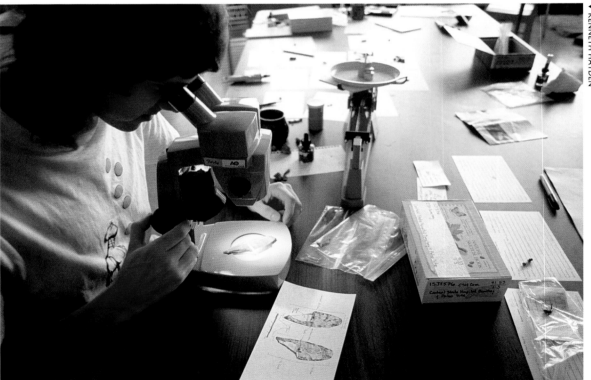

OUTSTANDING PUBLIC BUILDINGS and evocative statues stand out in Louisville. Gardencourt Mansion, one of the largest historic homes in the region, provides classrooms and offices for students and faculty at the Louisville Presbyterian Theological Seminary (ABOVE LEFT). A model of Rodin's *The Thinker* sets a good example for inquiring minds at the University of Louisville (TOP RIGHT), while the Temple of Love, located in Cavehill Cemetery, inspires all who see it (BOTTOM RIGHT AND OPPOSITE).

𝒯HOUGH PROUD OF ITS MODERATE climate, Louisville has four distinct seasons. *The Thinker* is an inspiration any time of year (OPPOSITE). Inclement weather occasionally tests the city's mettle, but it always brings out the best in Louisville's residents.

*I*NTERNATIONAL SYMBOL OF Louisville, the Thoroughbred racehorse contributes significantly to the local culture and economy.

*C*HURCHILL DOWNS DIGNITARIES: Along with horses, the Thorough-bred industry produces its share of winning personalities. Arthur Hancock, owner of Sunday Silence, shows off his four-leaf clover (BOTTOM LEFT). Nick Zito, Derby-winning trainer, gives an interview (BOTTOM RIGHT).

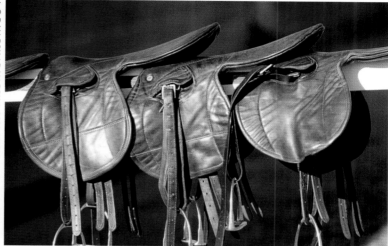

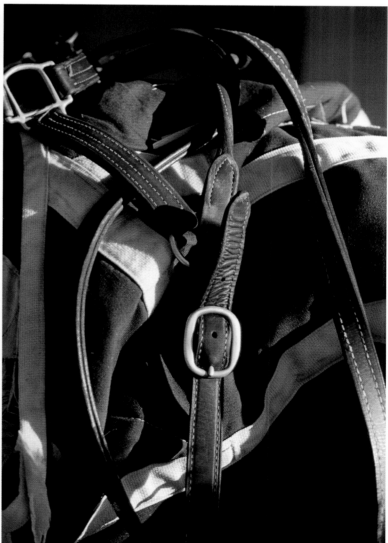

*M*UCH TIME IS SPENT GETTING Derby contenders ready to run for the roses.

*F*ROM FAST-BREAK BEGINNINGS TO furious finishes, Thoroughbred horse racing earns its reputation for relentless excitement with even the youngest of Louisvillians.

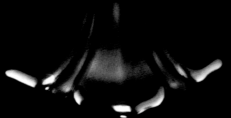

*T*HE KENTUCKY DERBY'S ENDURING symbols include a handful of roses, the winner's silver cup, and an annual parade of millinery creations.

*T*HE KENTUCKY DERBY IS MORE than a horse race. For two weeks preceding the event, Louisville celebrates in grand style with a swirl of balls, parties, and other treats for the senses.

*L*OUISVILLE IS A COLOR WHEEL OF activity, from balloon races to car shows and the annual state fair.

*N*ATURAL AND MAN-MADE LIGHT
compete for attention in the
vibrant night sky.

*B*Y HONORING THE DEAD—THROUGH
exhibition and memorials—Louisvillians demonstrate a reverence
for life, both past and present.
The area is known for the respect-
ful beauty of its cemeteries.

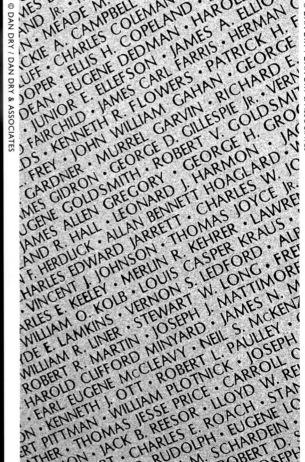

$\mathcal{B}$URLEY TOBACCO HAS LONG BEEN a staple crop for Kentucky farmers. The annual harvest and tobacco auction involve thousands of participants.

*L*OUISVILLE'S RICH HERITAGE IS preserved in rustic roadside scenes and historic sites like Locust Grove (TOP; BOTTOM RIGHT).

*L*OUISVILLIANS FROM ALL WALKS of life have mastered the art of casual elegance.

*W*ELCOMING ALL TYPES OF WEATHER,
sky-climbing trees grace Louisville
with shade and shelter.

*K*NOWN AS ONE OF THE NATION'S
most livable cities, Louisville's
greatest charm lies in its picturesque
neighborhoods.

ETHEL B. STOKE

ZELJKO CVIJANOVIC

JOHN NATION

JOHN NATION

𝒪NE CAN ONLY WONDER AT WHAT Claude Monet would have felt upon seeing Louisville's vast canvas of gardens.

*R*ESIDENTS ENJOY A FULL CALENDAR of beauty, as each season seems to outdo the others.

𝒯HE OHIO RIVER ISN'T THE ONLY
body of water in the Louisville
area. Nearby lakes provide both
recreation and tranquillity.

𝒜 KALEIDOSCOPE OF FALL IMAGES:
Autumn builds a world of yellow,
orange, and red as summer dwindles
from view.

*T*HE LOUISVILLE ZOO, NOTED FOR housing animals in natural habitats, is one of the finest zoological parks of its size in the nation and a popular getaway for children of all ages.

*L*OUISVILLE IS A CHILD'S PARADISE, from the wonders of the Louisville Science Center to the thrills of the Kentucky Kingdom Amusement Park (RIGHT).

Dozens of public pools provide cool entertainment during the heat of summer (OPPOSITE).

▼ PAUL B. BAYENS

▼ LYNN SHEA

A JOGGER TAKES HIS DAILY RUN across the timeless waters of the Ohio River (PAGES 134 AND 135).

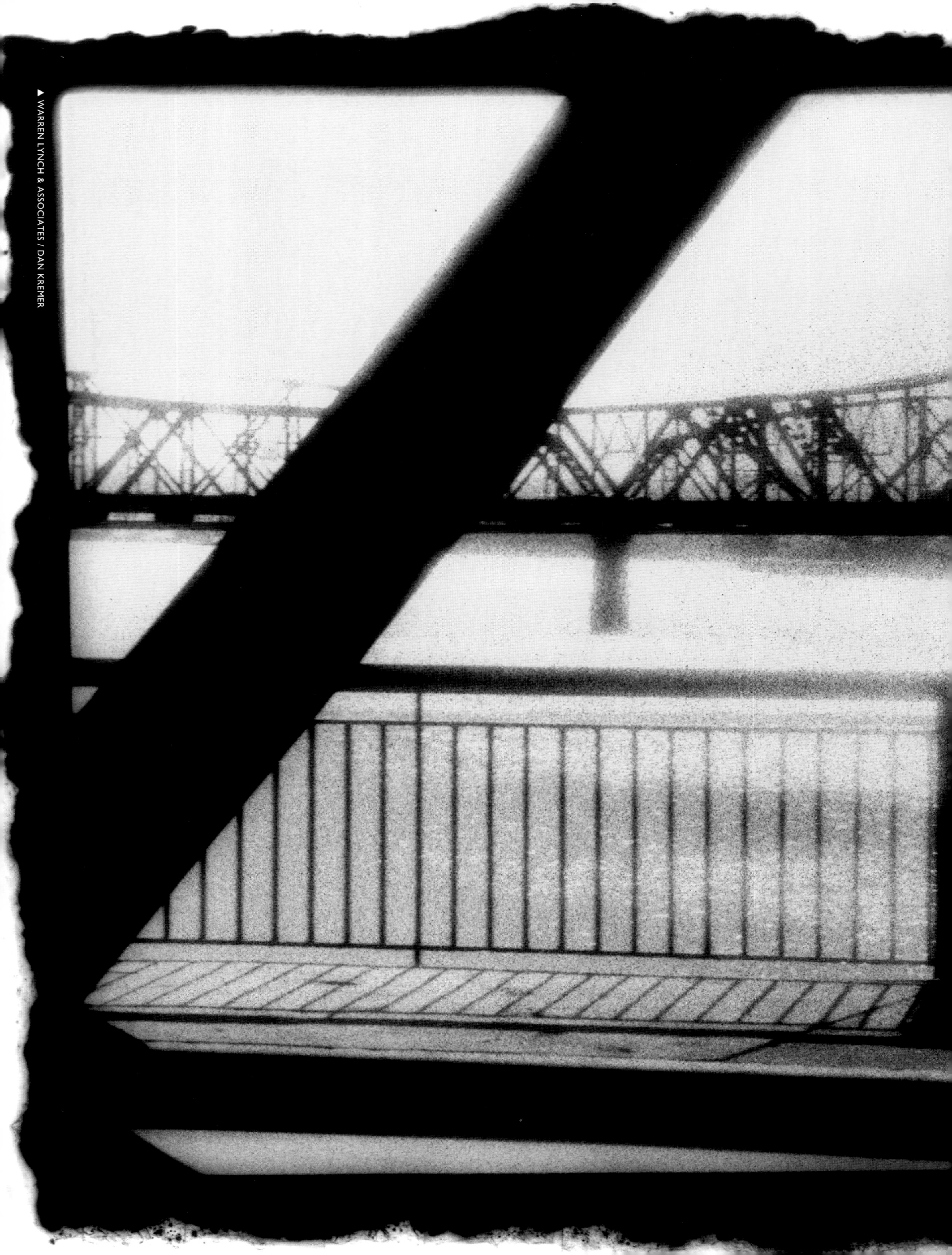

▲ WARREN LYNCH & ASSOCIATES / DAN KREMER

LOUIS

by WordWeavers, Inc.

VILLE

A LOOK AT THE CORPORATIONS, BUSINESSES, PROFESSIONAL GROUPS, AND COMMUNITY SERVICE ORGANIZATIONS THAT HAVE MADE THIS BOOK POSSIBLE. THEIR STORIES— OFFERING AN INFORMAL CHRONICLE OF THE LOCAL BUSINESS COMMUNITY—ARE ARRANGED ACCORDING TO THE DATE THEY WERE ESTABLISHED IN LOUISVILLE.

Acordia Personal ◆ ADVENT Environmental, Inc. ◆ Airguard Industries, Inc. ◆ Alliant Health System ◆ American Synthetic Rubber Corporation ◆ Ashland Inc. ◆ Bacons ◆ Bank One, Kentucky, NA ◆ Boehl Stopher & Graves ◆ Borden Inc. ◆ Brandeis Machinery and Supply Corporation ◆ Brown and Williamson Tobacco Corporation ◆ Brown-Forman Corporation ◆ Carrier Vibrating Equipment, Inc. ◆ Churchill Downs ◆ Columbia/HCA Healthcare Corporation ◆ Corhart Refractories Corporation ◆ Devoe & Raynolds Company ◆ Dixie Warehouse & Cartage Co. ◆ E.I. Du Pont de Nemours & Co. ◆ Fifth Third Bank ◆ GE Appliances ◆ Great Financial Bank, FSB ◆ Greater Louisville Economic Development Partnership ◆ J.J.B. Hilliard, W.L. Lyons, Inc. ◆ Humana, Inc. ◆ Hurstbourne Hotel and Conference Center ◆ Hyatt Regency Louisville ◆ Jim Beam Brands Company ◆ The Kroger Company ◆ LG&E Energy Corp. ◆ Louisville Area Chamber of Commerce ◆ Louisville Presbyterian Theological Seminary ◆ Luckett & Farley ◆ National City Bank Kentucky ◆ Philip Morris Companies Inc. ◆ Power Graphics, Inc. ◆ Providian Corporation ◆ Prudential Service Bureau, Inc. ◆ Publishers Printing Company ◆ Quartz Products Corporation ◆ RESCO RENTS ◆ Rohm and Haas Kentucky ◆ Sandvik Sorting Systems ◆ The Seelbach Hotel ◆ Spalding University ◆ Sullivan Colleges System ◆ Thornton Oil Corporation ◆ United Catalysts, Inc. ◆ University of Louisville ◆ WAVE 3 TV ◆ Wellness Institute, Inc. ◆ D.D. Williamson Group, Inc.

Profiles in Excellence

1 7 9 5

1929

A CASTING FROM AUGUSTE RODIN'S FAMOUS SCULPTURE *The Thinker* presides in front of Grawemeyer Hall at the University of Louisville. Originally created for the 1904 World's Fair in Paris, the unique piece, presented as a gift to the City of Louisville, serves today as a recognizable and impressive symbol of the university. ◆ Equally impressive as Rodin's

work is the long history of the University of Louisville. After nearly 200 years of teaching, research, and serving the community, U of L has established itself as one of the country's leading institutions of higher learning. Since its origin in 1798, shortly after the founding of the city and the commonwealth, U of L has grown to become Kentucky's second-largest university.

With a student population exceeding 21,000, U of L offers degrees in more than 175 fields of study. From its three campuses in Louisville and from teaching centers in Fort Knox and Madisonville, U of L contributes greatly to the economic and cultural vitality of Kentucky, serving as a major resource for health, engineering, education, business, technology, and research.

THE UNIVERSITY OF LOUISVILLE'S BEAUTIFUL PARKLIKE CAMPUS IS AN ATTRACTIVE PLACE FOR ITS MORE THAN 21,000 CULTURALLY DIVERSE STUDENTS.

▼ JONATHAN FLETCHER

Leading through Learning

The names of U of L alumni top many lists of civic and professional achievement. Through the years, the university has produced presidents of the American Medical Association, American Bar Association, American Dental Association, and many other professional societies.

Added to the numerous CEOs in business are the names of U.S. senators, Kentucky governors, and Louisville mayors who can trace their leadership roles to U of L. They join the many artists, writers, musicians, and other graduates who have left unique marks on the commonwealth and the nation. The Office of Development and Alumni has its hands full just keeping up with the school's more than 77,000 alumni.

Generations of leaders have chosen U of L as their center of learning due to the school's strong academic programs. Many U of L graduate and undergraduate programs are recognized by educators as models in shaping the growth of America. And, they reflect the depth and diversity of a faculty comprised of top scholars from around the world.

◄ JOHNATHAN FLETCHER

For instance, the Speed Scientific School educates engineers for tomorrow's world. The school's state-of-the-art facilities for rapid prototyping, materials research, factory automation, and computer-aided design/simulation, as well as student cooperative internships in industrial settings, offer future engineers the chance to participate in the cutting edge of technology.

Part of U of L's vision is to join the vanguard of developments in information technology by integrating data and data-processing hardware. U of L's Information Technology (IT) department has made a quantum leap toward that end during the past 10 years. IT utilizes a fiber-optic system to connect disparate components into a unified system and to empower individuals with technology at their desktops.

From an initial handful of computer operators, IT has evolved into almost 300 specialists, support staff, and student assistants distributed among 11 units, which handle everything from telephone installation to designing homepages for the World Wide Web.

Linking theory and practice, the College of Business and Public

Administration provides practical, hands-on experience joining students and faculty with business executives and managers from the public and private sectors. The college is unique in offering the nation's only four-year equine administration program. State-of-the-art technologies bring global information to the classroom and connect students with people throughout the world. The Integrated MBA program sets a standard for a learning-centered, practical, and entrepreneur-focused program in a unique two-year, part-time educational experience.

U of L's academic strength carries over into its athletic programs. It is the only university to win national championships in both debate and basketball, and, as two-time NCAA Division I champions, the basketball Cardinals hold the record for the longest winning tradition in basketball, going 46 years between losing seasons.

A History of Community Service
Throughout its history, U of L has played a pivotal role in the Louisville community. For ex-

ample, the Health Sciences Center provides millions of dollars each year in uncompensated patient and indigent care through the University of Louisville Hospital. Area residents receive the benefit of some of the most advanced therapies for a host of medical and dental needs.

And, the hospital houses Kentucky's first Level I trauma center, with a 24-hour emergency helicopter service, Statflight. The trauma center was one of the first of its kind in the country and is consistently ranked as one of the nation's best.

Another $1 million of social work services is provided without fee by the Kent School of Social Work as part of its training practicum. The School of Education has provided training and assistance for area schools in implementing the state's innovative educational reforms.

By their investment in U of L, individual and corporate residents of Kentucky help create an educated and productive workforce, in addition to tax revenue and a robust economy. Partnerships

such as the Telecommunications Research Center, formed with U of L, the state, and Bell South, put technology to progressive use in support of distance learning and commercial applications.

U of L's new president, John Shumaker, has reason to be confident about the road ahead. He now oversees a vibrant metropolitan university that is focused on the future and that continues to be an outstanding source of ideas, competence, and imagination for Louisville, all of Kentucky, and the surrounding region.

A SCENIC CAMPUS SETTING ENCOURAGES LEARNING AMONG THE UNIVERSITY'S STUDENTS WHO CAN EARN DEGREES IN MORE THAN 175 FIELDS OF STUDY (ABOVE).

CELEBRATING ITS 1994 METRO CONFERENCE WIN, THE LOUISVILLE CARDINALS TEAM HOLDS THE NATIONAL RECORD FOR POSTING 46 WINNING SEASONS (LEFT).

A LETTER FROM PRESIDENT BILL CLINTON DATED JANUARY 4, 1995, states, "Jim Beam Distilling Company has prospered because of the dedication and commitment of its hardworking employees, who exemplify the very best of American labor and know-how." The president's letter acknowledges what millions of customers and six generations of the Beam family have known

so well: that Jim Beam Bourbon, the best-selling bourbon whiskey in the world, is also one of the finest.

Part of American History

The Jim Beam story goes back more than 200 years to family patriarch Jacob Beam, who settled in Kentucky in 1788, the same year the U. S. Constitution was ratified. Jacob Beam found in

TOURISTS ENJOY A CARRIAGE RIDE THROUGH SCENIC LOUISVILLE, HOME TO JIM BEAM BRANDS COMPANY, DISTILLER OF BEST-SELLING JIM BEAM BOURBON.

Kentucky a bountiful land blessed with fertile soil, ample rain, and free-flowing spring-water—the perfect ingredients for growing corn. In 1795 he began fermenting corn and other grains according to a still-secret recipe to make an outstanding bourbon whiskey.

Bourbon—a special kind of whiskey native to America—was an important part of the pioneer life. "In frontier days, whiskey was better than money as a medium of exchange; in times of inflation you could always drink it yourself—and by the time you finished the first barrel, the inflationary cycle prob-ably would be over," Jacob Beam's great-great-grandson, T. Jeremiah Beam, once said. Indeed, many early American anecdotes associate bourbon whiskey and leaders of the period, such as George Washington, Davy Crockett, Daniel Webster, and Abraham Lincoln.

Jacob Beam passed on his bourbon-making expertise to his son, David. Thus began a family tradition that continues to this day. David's son, David M. Beam, moved the distillery from its origi-nal Bourbon County home to Nelson County, Kentucky, just south of Louisville.

His son, James Beauregard Beam—the Jim Beam for whom the distillery is named—started making bourbon in 1880 and, during his 67 years at the helm of the family business, turned the distillery into an internationally renowned organization. He was followed by T. Jeremiah Beam in 1947. During the time that Jeremiah served as master distiller, he re-established the old American

custom of producing special com-memorative whiskey flasks, includ-ing those marking the admission of Alaska and Hawaii to the Union and observing the centennials of many other states. These bottles generated a collecting craze and the formation of "Beam clubs."

The Strength of Tradition

In 1960 Jeremiah Beam brought his nephew, Booker Noe Jr., into the family business. Today, Noe serves as master distiller emeritus. Under his tutelage, the distillery continues to use the same vintage yeast strain created by the com-pany in 1934. Noe keeps a copy of the secret bourbon formula in a Bardstown bank.

Though Jim Beam Bourbon has always had many loyal followers, Noe notes with pride that a new generation has developed an appre-ciation for its 200-year American history. "It's wonderful to see people today enjoying the same thing that their parents and grandparents en-joyed years before them," he says. "I'm proud to see other families sharing and passing down the same enjoyment for Jim Beam Bourbon that has been passed down in the Beam family for 200 years."

© DAN DRY / DAN DRY & ASSOCIATES

In 1995 one of Louisville's most viable and time-tested financial institutions, Liberty National Bank and Trust Company, assumed a new name: Bank One, Kentucky, NA. The bank is the Kentucky arm of BANC ONE CORPORATION, one of the largest financial institutions in the country. The two banks merged in 1994, uniting Liberty's longstanding commitment to

innovation and community with of one of America's strongest financial institutions.

Now one of the largest banks in Kentucky—with assets of more than $7 billion—Bank One, Kentucky began as the German Insurance Company in 1854. The bank, which was chartered separately from the insurance company in 1872, took the name Liberty in 1918 in response to American patriotism efforts during World War I. In 1935 Liberty became a national bank.

In the decades that followed, the bank developed a reputation as an innovative provider of financial services. In 1942 it was the first bank in Louisville to offer a pay-as-you-go checking account. In 1971 Liberty installed the first automated teller machines in Kentucky. The bank introduced discount brokerage services to customers and correspondent banks in 1983. In keeping with its spirit of banking innova-

tions, in 1995 Bank One offered the first 100 percent equity lending product in Louisville.

In every case Bank One's predecessor successfully applied a marketer's touch and a customer orientation to the staid world of banking. The bank experienced rapid growth in the 1980s and early 1990s in part by acquiring banks in Owensboro, Hopkinsville, Elizabethtown, Shelbyville, Lexington, and southern Indiana.

Now, as Bank One, it operates 112 banking centers in Kentucky and southern Indiana, 42 of which are located in the Louisville metro area. The bank is a comprehensive provider of financial services, offering a wide range of retail and commercial banking products. Bank One also provides credit life insurance, leasing, brokerage, check processing, and retail loan services through several nonbanking subsidiaries.

A service philosophy also governs Bank One's role in the community. "Our people give their time, both personally and professionally," says Malcolm B. Chancey Jr., the bank's chairman and CEO. These efforts have translated into thousands of volunteer hours for a variety of causes and organizations, including Metro United Way, Fund for the Arts, Kentucky Center for the Arts, Falls of the Ohio Visitor Center, Kentucky Derby Festival, and Jefferson County Public Schools. The bank also has a long tradition to contributing time and money to civic projects.

By combining business savvy with good corporate citizenship, Bank One has earned its place among Louisville's top financial institutions.

BANK ONE OFFERS A WIDE VARIETY OF FINANCIAL SERVICES THAT PROVIDE A PERSONAL TOUCH FOR ITS CUSTOMERS (ABOVE).

BANK ONE HAS 112 BANKING CENTERS IN KENTUCKY AND SOUTHERN INDIANA, 42 OF THEM IN THE LOUISVILLE METRO AREA, INCLUDING THIS ONE IN ST. MATTHEWS (LEFT).

LG&E ENERGY CORP.

*A*LTHOUGH ITS ROOTS EXTEND BACK MORE THAN 150 YEARS as one of America's oldest utilities, Louisville Gas and Electric Company (LG&E) and its parent company, LG&E Energy Corp., now rank among the most innovative and forward-looking energy services companies in the nation. LG&E Energy has grown from its founding as a small local utility into a recognized national leader of electric and natural gas services with global operations.

The company's earliest predecessor, the Louisville Gas and Water Company, was incorporated in 1838 to provide light for the streets, homes, and businesses of a few thousand citizens. At that time, the utility simply manufactured, distributed, and sold gas to the Louisville area.

However, today's energy industry is much more complex. The company serves hundreds of thousands of retail and wholesale electric and natural gas customers in markets spanning thousands of miles throughout Metro Louisville, the United States, Argentina, and Spain.

This impressive growth has come amid the most sweeping changes in the energy services industry. The company anticipated and embraced the economic and deregulatory forces reshaping its industry and marketplace today, and this preparation enabled it to capitalize on those changes.

Strategic Alignment

LG&E Energy Corp. has reshaped itself from a traditional, vertically integrated utility into four diverse energy services divisions that focus on distribution services, gas marketing, power marketing, and power generation. These divisions improve customer responsiveness, speed decision making, and focus on the needs of the supply, marketing, and distribution segments of the current industry.

LG&E, LG&E Energy Corp.'s local utility company, serves more than 346,100 electric and 272,200 natural gas customers in a territory covering 700 square miles in 17 Kentucky counties. It provides gas and electric energy to industrial, commercial, and residential customers at rates that are among the nation's lowest.

Some analysts and industry executives consider the company a rising star in the energy industry and a model for other utilities. Standard & Poor's places LG&E among the 25 utilities best positioned to cope with deregulation. And Resource Data International, Inc. in Boulder, Colorado, has rated LG&E among the nation's most competitive utilities. A recent management audit of the utility done at the request of the Public Service Commission of Kentucky found that LG&E is an industry leader with superior skills in identifying and implementing performance improvements.

The company owns, has partnership interests in, or operates 14 power plants throughout the United States, including four in the Louisville area. International projects, including a natural gas plant in Argentina and a wind plant in Spain, are further evidence of the company's ability to develop and manage a variety of power projects in diverse markets. It has sales offices in key cities throughout the United States and Canada. It also established one of the nation's first power-marketing companies, which has quickly risen to a leading position, marketing power to other utilities, municipalities, and rural cooperatives throughout the United States.

The addition in 1995 of Hadson Gas Services, Inc., a natural gas marketer, now positions the company to offer integrated natural gas and electric energy products on a national basis. The acquisition brought storage facilities, processing plants, and 1,300 miles of gas-gathering systems in New Mexico, Texas, Oklahoma, and Montana into the company. The company is

ELECTRICITY FOR THE LOUISVILLE METROPOLITAN AREA IS PRODUCED AT THREE SCRUBBER-EQUIPPED, COAL-FIRED PLANTS, INCLUDING THE TRIMBLE COUNTY GENERATING STATION (RIGHT).

CORPORATE OFFICES FOR LG&E ENERGY CORP. AND LOUISVILLE GAS AND ELECTRIC COMPANY ARE IN THE LG&E BUILDING ON HISTORIC MAIN STREET (BELOW).

positioned to be among the first businesses to offer electric and natural gas marketing on a national level.

Making Louisville a Cleaner Place to Live

While growing into a national player, the company continues to invest in the quality of its operations in Louisville. LG&E continues to add clean-burning natural gas vehicles to its fleet. It installed scrubbers to remove sulfur dioxide from its emissions years ahead of most utilities. In fact, LG&E's scrubber research and refinements have earned national and international awards and recognition.

But LG&E's accomplishments go far beyond awards. The utility's pollution-control efforts helped Jefferson County reach attainment status for sulfur dioxide in 1985. The U.S. Environmental Protection Agency's approval of that status lessened restrictions on business growth and expansion.

An Energetic Educator and Community Leader

In 1989 LG&E assumed a more prominent educational role in the community through the Environmental Tech Prep program at Valley High School. LG&E and the Jefferson County Public Schools collaborated to develop a curriculum, establish an environmental laboratory, and supply the necessary resource material. This nationally recognized program helps students develop personally, academically, and professionally.

LG&E also supports other educational programs and community organizations, including the Kerrick Elementary School's Nature Kingdom, the science enrichment program at Robert Frost Middle School, Metro United Way and Junior Achievement of Kentuckiana.

Community Leadership

LG&E Energy Corp. employees at every level serve on boards and in other leadership positions for a wide variety of civic, charitable, and religious organizations such as chambers of commerce, economic development agencies, Metro United Way, and church and youth groups.

The utility and its employees also partner with the Kentuckiana Minority Supplier Development Council to promote business opportunities for minority-owned businesses.

LG&E Energy Corp. employees also financially support many educational, civic, and charitable organizations. In addition, the company's LG&E Energy Foundation Inc. provides financial support to many of these same organizations as well as others like them in communities where the company does business.

Ultimately, the success of LG&E Energy Corp. will be measured by all its constituents, including its customers and shareholders. The company is firmly committed to earning the trust of these stakeholders as it continues to act on its vision of the future.

ELECTRIC SERVICE DELIVERY CREWS ARE ALWAYS IMPROVING LOUISVILLE GAS AND ELECTRIC COMPANY'S DISTRIBUTION SYSTEM THROUGHOUT ITS SERVICE TERRITORY.

NATURAL GAS SERVICE AND PRODUCTS ARE CONSTANTLY BEING EXPANDED AS THE LOUISVILLE METROPOLITAN AREA CONTINUES TO GROW. NEW NATURAL GAS SERVICE LINES ARE COLOR-CODED YELLOW FOR EASIER IDENTIFICATION.

OUISVILLE COMBINES MANY OF THE ADVANTAGES OF BIG CITY living with the friendly disposition of a small town. Shoppers have long recognized Bacons department store as a local business that offers both the personal service of a hometown retailer and the wide selection and cosmopolitan atmosphere of a big city department store. Having served the Louisville area for 150

years, the company continues to live up to this reputation.

"We're the local leader in fashion, home furnishings, and other retail segments," says Bacons President Thomas N. Groh. Indeed, Bacons was voted the city's top department store in a 1995 poll sponsored by *Louisville Magazine*.

Furnishing Louisville for 150 Years

Bacons began in 1845 as J. Bacon & Sons Company. The small retail operation founded by Jeremiah Bacon grew rapidly to become a successful business, adding a wholesale component in 1876. Shortly after the turn of the century, Bacons moved into a large, new building in the heart of downtown Louisville.

The store, which was under the direction of the founder's three sons, was sold in 1903. In 1914 Mercantile Stores Company, Inc.— then based in Wilmington, Delaware—acquired the Louisville business and has remained its parent company ever since.

Today, Mercantile is headquar-

tered in Fairfield, Ohio. A large department store retailer operating 105 stores in 13 chains across 17 states, the company is typically among the top organizations in its industry in per-square-foot sales.

Mercantile—which took in more than $2.5 billion in sales in 1994—prides itself on the allegiance of longtime employees. In addition, the company encourages initiative and high-quality customer service in all its people. This customer-first

philosophy is identical to the one that drives Bacons. "We have more than 2,500 Louisville-area employees," says Bacons Operations Director Howard Hogue. "Providing service is the reason they come to work each day."

Building on a Service Tradition
Bacons is accessible to every population in the Kentuckiana area through stores at seven locations, including Mall St.

THE BASHFORD MANOR MALL STORE FOR THE HOME IS ONE OF SEVEN BACONS LOCATIONS (FAR RIGHT).

BACONS' MALL ST. MATTHEWS LOCATION OPENED IN 1988 TO SERVE EASTERN JEFFERSON COUNTY AND OLDHAM COUNTY SUBURBAN AREAS (BELOW).

Matthews, Shively, St. Matthews Store for the Home, Bashford Manor Mall, River Falls Mall in Southern Indiana, Bashford Manor Mall Store for the Home, and the Louisville Galleria. The success of the Galleria store has been particularly gratifying. Bacons is pleased to play an important role in the shopping mall that has helped revitalize the retail trade in downtown Louisville.

Aside from convenient locations, Bacons can boast of having some of the most loyal customers in the region. The department store chain—which has been serving many Louisville families for generations—is appreciated as a familiar part of the local landscape. Long-time Bacons shoppers look forward to a variety of seasonal sales and exciting promotions that guarantee good value.

Bacons has also expanded to offer its customers even more choices in keeping with its tradition of excellent service. In recent years,

the company has begun to aggressively acquire and remodel properties with an eye to upscale markets. For example, an old storefront in Mall St. Matthews, purchased in 1987, is now a Bacons store selling exclusively men's and women's clothing, shoes, cosmetics, and other accessories—all ready to wear.

Bacons has opened two other niche stores: the Home Stores in St. Matthews and in Bashford Manor Mall. These facilities feature full lines of furniture, carpet, linens, draperies, housewares, and other furnishings. The Home Stores carry just about everything a customer needs to furnish or redecorate the home.

It is no accident that Bacons has dedicated two sites to home furnishings. The company made this strategic move based on the fact that low interest rates and a recovering economy have stimulated home buying, which, in turn, has resulted in growing consumer interest in furniture and other items. This trend, which should continue for

some time, makes it possible for a department store retailer such as Bacons to successfully target particular market segments with strong products and value.

Carrying On in a Successful Fashion

Bacons' 150th anniversary in 1995 demonstrated the retailer's lasting vigor. It remains the first stop in Louisville for both quality private label fashions like 955 and Signature Expressions, and prominent designer labels like Esteé Lauder, Lancome, Clinique, Liz Claiborne, Calvin Klein, Nautica, and many more.

According to Groh, traditional strengths like fashion and innovations like the Home Stores will keep Bacons in the forefront of Kentuckiana department stores for years to come. He adds, "We want to be as much a part of Louisville's future as we've been part of its past."

DISCERNING SHOPPERS WILL FIND CLOTHES FOR EVERY OCCASION AT THE RALPH LAUREN POLO SHOP FOR MEN (LEFT) OR THE DESIGNER COLLECTION FOR WOMEN (RIGHT) IN BACONS' MALL ST. MATTHEWS LOCATION.

EQUIP THE SAINTS FOR THE WORK OF MINISTRY," WAS PAUL'S instruction to the Ephesians in the New Testament. At Louisville Presbyterian Theological Seminary, "Equipping the Saints" is the theme for the school's fund-raising and expansion program as it nears its 150th anniversary. ♦ The Seminary has always been a strong voice in the local, national, and international community

and has plans to become an even broader ecumenical and interfaith resource in the future. Its primary goal remains equipping students, clergy, and laypeople for Christian leadership.

A Unique and Progressive Tradition

One of the country's oldest theological institutions, Louisville Seminary has a unique history and mission. Founded in 1853, the current Seminary resulted from a 1901 merger between Danville Seminary of Danville, Kentucky, and Louisville Presbyterian Theological Seminary. The two institutions represented two streams of the Presbyterian Church, which were formally united in the 1980s thanks in no small part to efforts by Seminary leaders.

Historically, the Seminary has supported the Louisville community in many ways. The Seminary's former 1st and Broadway campus provided shelter for those forced from their homes during the 1937 flood and for returning veterans from World War II. In the 1940s the Seminary's field education program began providing pastors, chaplains, and counselors to churches, hospitals, and social agencies in the region.

In recent years the City of Louisville and Louisville Seminary joined forces to raise nearly $7 million to renovate the historic mansion, Gardencourt, on the current Seminary campus on Alta Vista Road. The renovation was recognized with a Preservation Alliance Award in 1991. While providing classrooms and offices for the Seminary, the beautiful facility has be-

come a popular meeting place for area corporations, charitable organizations, and social events. Additionally, Louisville and the Seminary were partners in recruiting the Presbyterian Church (U.S.A.) national offices to Louisville, a move that brought thousands of jobs and a major resource for members of the community.

Long known for its progressive mission, the Seminary in the 1950s began welcoming women and African-Americans to its student body. Today the Louisville Seminary offers opportunities not found at most other theological schools. Its highly successful Marriage and Family Therapy Program is one of only four accredited, seminary-affiliated

programs in the United States. "The marriage and family therapy program prepares students to become therapists who specialize in family-related issues while drawing on the resources of Christian tradition and spirituality," according to Professor of Pastoral Theology Dr. Nancy J. Ramsay. "This is just one of the ways our students are preparing to support families and reinforce the work of the church, making it relevant in today's society."

Field education is an integral part of the Seminary's program. "Students here have opportunities to do field education throughout their time at the Seminary," says Seminary President John M. Mulder. "Ministry students may work as worship assistants in large congregations or small parishes, as chaplains at medical facilities, and as counselors in the community." Students at Louisville Seminary are also involved in nearly all aspects of the institution's operations, worship, and governance. "We want to prepare people to be leaders and take an active part involving the health and well-being of their communities," explains Dean of Students the Reverend Donna Melloan.

Louisville Seminary is also a visible supporter of scholarly research into religious issues. With the University of Louisville, the Seminary cosponsors the Grawemeyer Award in Religion, an international award of $150,000 honoring people whose work explores the relationship between human beings and the divine. The Seminary's Louisville Institute—an education and research program funded by the Lilly Endowment, Inc.—supports religious research in American culture through grants and conferences.

Equipping the Saints for the Next Century

Continuing its energetic approach to its mission, Louisville Seminary has initiated a major effort—Equipping the Saints: The 150th Anniversary Project. Along with

campus renovations, more student aid, and endowed teaching positions, the project includes new programs to help the Seminary lead efforts to make the Christian church part of everyday life.

"One of the most exciting parts of the plan is the new Louisville Center for Christian Formation," says Vice President for Development Larry Hitner. "It will be a specialized program to help students, congregations, parents, and youth learn how to live and transmit the faith in family life. There is no comparable program at any other mainline Protestant seminary in the country."

In its efforts to continue embracing diversity, another key part of the Seminary's strategic plan is its Ministry Across Cultures. "This program will give all master's-level students the opportunity to gain field experience within different cultures through immersion trips to Latin America, Europe, Asia, Appalachia, or the inner city," says Seminary Dean W. Eugene March.

Along with this program, the Seminary is establishing a scholars fund called New Horizons to support students who need it most, as well as a fellowship to increase the

presence of racial-ethnic professors for future leadership. The Seminary is also planning to increase the number of international students on campus to further broaden the perspectives available for all students.

Finally, to support its expanded role as a place for retreat and study, the Seminary is building short-term, on-campus lodging for guests who come for seminars, conferences, or independent study.

The goal of the 150th Anniversary Project is to raise more than $43 million. The project will be completed by 2003, exactly 150 years after the Seminary's founding. Long after the project is finished, Louisville Seminary will still be fulfilling its mission of preparing visionary leadership for the community of faith.

WORSHIPERS SPILL OUT ONTO THE LOUISVILLE SEMINARY QUADRANGLE AFTER A MORNING SERVICE IN CALDWELL CHAPEL (TOP).

DR. MARTY SOARDS, PROFESSOR OF NEW TESTAMENT, DRIVES A POINT HOME USING GREEK TEXT IN HIS GALATIANS CLASS (BOTTOM).

LUCKETT & FARLEY

*I*T IS NOT UNUSUAL FOR AN ARCHITECTURAL FIRM TO DESIGN A structure that eventually becomes a landmark. However, it is unusual for an architectural firm to have created so many landmarks that the firm itself becomes a landmark. So it is with Luckett & Farley. ♦ From the Twin Spires of Churchill Downs to the South Wing of the Kentucky Fair & Exposition Center, Luckett & Farley has been responsible for creating

many of Louisville's most recognized buildings.

A Rich History

Luckett & Farley is one of the oldest continuing architectural firms in the country, beginning its tradition in 1853. Under the names of Rogers & Henry Whitestone, and subsequently, D. X. Murphy and Brother, the firm designed some of Louisville's most enduring landmarks in the late 1800s. These include the Twin Spires of Churchill Downs, the Louisville City Hall Clock Tower, the original Jefferson County Jail, the L&N Office Building, the church and rectory of St. Bonafice, St. Anthony's Hospital, and the original Galt House Hotel.

In 1962 the owners of the firm, Jean D. Farley and T.D. Luckett, changed the firm's name as

well as the scope of its practice. Through its evolution, Luckett & Farley's staff included architects, along with civil and structural engineers. By 1970 the firm also provided in-house mechanical and electrical engineering services.

This unique structure, com-

bined with the firm's history of innovative designs, led to Luckett & Farley's success in designing high-profile projects in the midst of ever-increasing competition. These projects included the South Wing of the Kentucky Fair & Exposition Center, additions to the Ford Ken-

tucky Truck Plant, the Kentucky Farm Bureau headquarters, and the Bank One Building in New Albany, Indiana.

A Single Source

Today, Luckett & Farley is a total design firm offering comprehensive services through a diverse staff, including professionals in architecture; mechanical, plumbing, electrical, structural, and civil engineering; interior design and space planning; and program and construction management. Areas of focus for these services are clients in the health care, industrial, education, commercial, and government sectors.

Changing with the Marketplace

"We change with the marketplace," says Dennis DeWitt, president of the 142-year-old company. That, he adds, is the main reason for Luckett & Farley's success.

"I think the main reason the firm has survived is that it has remained flexible in responding to the

marketplace," says DeWitt. "As client expectations and the market conditions have changed, the firm's services and approach have changed."

Flexibility and Innovation

Being a hometown company and having a colorful history does not automatically translate to success. Flexibility and innovation are additional qualities that have led to Luckett & Farley's success. The firm's management foresaw the decline in the number of public projects and made the decision to diversify into industrial and institutional work in addition to construction management. This move paved the way for projects such as the Ford Kentucky truck plant; the General Motors R&D facility in Bedford, Indiana; and nationwide hospital projects for Vencor and Columbia/HCA.

Exceeding the Client's Expectations

Luckett & Farley believes that a successful design should exceed the client's expectations. The firm views each project as a unique opportunity. Extensive up-front meetings during the early stages of design allow the firm to zero in on the client's needs, while enabling Luckett & Farley staff to weave their own ideas into the

project. The result is a structure that exceeds the client's expectations in both form and function.

Ron Kendall, senior vice president, says, "While other firms can perform successfully as single disciplines, our firm has found its strength in providing a complete design service in a single organization. This approach is the way our people perform most effectively."

That's probably why the firm has maintained a repeat-business record exceeding 80 percent annually—a statistic that is a landmark in itself.

OTHER LUCKETT & FARLEY PROJECTS INCLUDE (CLOCKWISE FROM ABOVE) KENTUCKY FARM BUREAU'S HEADQUARTERS, ERNST & YOUNG'S OFFICES, VENCOR HOSPITAL'S INDIANAPOLIS ICU, AND BANK ONE OF NEW ALBANY, INDIANA.

HEADQUARTERED IN LOUISVILLE, NATIONAL CITY BANK, Kentucky—through its 101 branch offices in Kentucky and southern Indiana—provides a full range of banking services to retail and commercial customers. A $7.4 billion member bank of National City Corporation in Cleveland, Ohio, the bank serves 29 communities and employs more than 2,900 people. ◆ The product

of a merger brought about by the turbulent economic climate of the 1980s and the deregulation of the banking industry, National City Bank is an institution dedicated to being more competitive in this new banking environment and to maintaining its superior record of performance.

First National Bank of Louisville, the local predecessor to National City Bank, became part of the $50 billion National City Corporation in 1988. National City Corporation is celebrating its 150th anniversary this year and holds the number one deposit market share in the combined three-state area of Indiana, Kentucky, and Ohio. The corporation's capital ratio (the amount of money the bank has on hand) is one of the highest among America's top 50 banks.

A Prestigious History

It's been a long road to the achievement of such a leadership position, both in Louisville and the nation. National City Bank,

◀ JOHN LAIR

Kentucky owes its beginnings to the foresight and vision of 35 men and three women who, on September 7, 1863, applied for a national banking charter with a proposed total investment of $110,000. Forty-five days later, on October 22, First National Bank of Louisville opened for business, bringing prestige to the city for having the first "national" bank south of the Mason-Dixon Line.

The bank prospered and grew through hard times, including the Civil War and World War I. Even when the country was in the midst of the Great Depression, the bank remained among the strongest in the nation. As First National Bank, it acquired the majority of the deposits from a large Kentucky bank that had failed, thus freeing the accounts of those depositors and providing much needed relief to the community.

Always a community leader, the bank remained strong throughout the 1930s and 1940s, despite the effects of the depression and the onslaught of World War II. By the end of the war, First National Bank

had more than 300 employees and was considered one of the top banking institutions in the state.

Always a Leader in Technology

The next two decades were very prosperous for the company. The 1950s brought recognition to its trust business, as it grew to become the largest in the state. And the 1960s represented a time of innovation when more than 60,000 checking accounts were converted to an electronic data processing system.

The 1970s brought an air of change and expansion to the bank, as the branch system grew tremendously and automatic teller machines (ATMs) were introduced. In 1979 the bank created National Processing Company. It is now the largest credit card processing company in the nation and is the only processor of airline tickets for travel agents.

After more than 150 years of growth and prosperity, National City Bank is poised to leap into the new century, while still providing the personal touch of a committed local community banking system.

D.D. Williamson & Co., Inc.

THE LARGEST MANUFACTURER OF CARAMEL COLORING IN THE world, Louisville-based D.D. Williamson & Co., Inc. was founded in 1865 as a producer of flavoring extracts. In its early days, D.D. Williamson served the brewery industry. But in 1919, when Prohibition was enacted, the company was faced with the challenge of retooling its products for a new market. D.D. Williamson turned to the food industry and became the major supplier of caramel coloring to the soft drink market—a segment of the industry that today accounts for 70 percent of the company's sales.

Today, D.D. Williamson produces more than 50 varieties of caramel coloring in liquid and powdered forms for use in baked goods, alcoholic beverages, soups, sauces, frozen foods, pharmaceuticals, dry product mixes, and pet foods.

Global Reach

Through an aggressive global-market strategy, D.D. Williamson maintains production facilities in Louisville; Modesto, California; Gurabo, Puerto Rico; and Cork, Ireland. With 120 employees worldwide, D.D. Williamson generates 60 percent of its sales outside the United States.

Its Louisville headquarters includes a caramel color plant, a complete analytical research and development laboratory, a fully equipped applications laboratory, a regional sales office, and a warehouse. From its Louisville location, D.D. Williamson ships caramel color to food and beverage manufacturers around the world.

The Modesto operation produces and warehouses caramel colors for customers in the western United States and throughout the Pacific Basin. The Cork facility includes a caramel color plant; applications laboratory; regional sales office; and a warehouse for serving food processors throughout Europe, the Middle East, and Africa. Gurabo is home to the newest D.D. Williamson caramel color plant, which handles the specialized needs of Puerto Rico and its Caribbean neighbors.

Since 1987 D.D. Williamson has supported its global presence with a quality improvement process focusing on customers, associates, suppliers, shareholders, and the local community. This team-based program has caused tremendous forward strides in the company's dedication to manufacturing and service excellence. For example, D.D. Williamson (Ireland) was certified by the International Organization for Standardization as ISO 9002 in 1991.

Community Outreach

D.D. Williamson's community outreach efforts are an integral part of its business. The company boasts 100 percent participation in the Louisville Metro United Way Campaign, making it one of the campaign's top five organizations in per capita contributions. This generosity extends to other causes, as well.

D.D. Williamson has achieved worldwide leadership in an essential segment of the food industry. That leadership is a source of both pride and continuous improvement for the company—the ingredients for success.

D.D. WILLIAMSON PRODUCES MORE THAN 50 VARIETIES OF CARAMEL COLORING IN LIQUID AND POWDERED FORMS FOR USE IN BAKED GOODS, ALCOHOLIC BEVERAGES, SOUPS, SAUCES, FROZEN FOODS, PHARMACEUTICALS, DRY PRODUCT MIXES, AND PET FOODS.

ESTLED IN THE FOOTHILLS JUST 20 MILES SOUTH OF LOUISVILLE LIES the town of Shepherdsville, Kentucky. Although small in stature, Shepherdsville can boast of being home to one of the largest and most technologically advanced printing operations in North America, Publishers Printing Company. A family-owned and -operated business for more than 125 years, Publishers is dedicated to being the best printing

resource there is for professional magazines and journals.

High-Tech Capabilities; Hometown Service

Publishers' small-town setting belies its visionary outlook and high-tech capabilities. The company's 1,600 employees handle an impressive array of more than 400 trade and special-interest publications, as well as several city magazines and a number of well-known consumer publications. Their determination to attain the finest standards in the printing industry has rewarded them with a highly satisfied clientele, an exclusive group that has shared in Publishers' successful growth, which averages around 15 percent per year.

"What's made our company unique is the niche carved out by my father in the 1950s and 1960s," says company Executive Vice President Michael J. Simon. "And, we plow nearly 100 percent of the profits back into our business to maintain our technological edge."

Most recently, the company became the first printer in the world to use direct-to-plate printing of an entire four-color magazine. This is a revolutionary new process in which printing is done without the use of film negatives. Designers simply send visuals and page-layout files to Publishers on diskette, and they can then view electronic proofs on their own monitors in a matter of days.

Publishers invested more than half a million dollars in the most technologically advanced equipment to reach this level of performance. It took months of installation, training, and testing but the company thinks it's worth the effort. "We feel that

direct-to-plate makes a lot of sense," Simon insists. "When you eliminate consumables like film you can reduce costs and pass the savings on to your client."

Rich in History and Traditions

Aside from its commitment to high quality, outstanding service, and leading-edge technology, Publishers is most distinguished by its history. Started in 1866 in Louisville, Publishers Printing began as a German-Catholic newspaper, guided by Nicholas Simon.

Born in 1823, Nicholas Simon was raised in Albersweiler, Germany, a town that dates back to the reign of Charlemagne. Albersweiler had a deep sense of history and culture that Nicholas Simon was never to forget, even after he moved to the United States in 1846.

Nicholas Simon began his life

in America as a shoemaker and then served his new country in both the Mexican and Civil wars. After leaving the army in 1866, he purchased an interest in a newly formed German newspaper in Louisville. The company became the Printing Rooms of Nicholas Simon.

He worked with his two sons, John and Frank X., and under his leadership the firm expanded into the commercial field, including advertising for local merchants, dance programs, elaborate business cards, and various invitations. In 1879, a newspaper for the Catholic Archdiocese of Louisville was established, called the *Record*. Nicholas Simon was awarded the contract, and the company continued to print this publication for 74 years.

When Nicholas retired in 1880, his sons operated the business as a partnership until 1885.

CLOCKWISE FROM RIGHT: PHOTO TAKEN IN 1990 OF FRANK E. SIMON (CENTER), FLANKED BY SONS NICHOLAS (LEFT) AND MICHAEL, PRIOR TO FRANK'S DEATH. NICK IS NOW PRESIDENT, AND MICHAEL IS EXECUTIVE VICE PRESIDENT.

PUBLISHERS PRINTING COMPANY HAS 17 WEB OFFSET PRESSES, WHICH COLLECTIVELY USE MORE THAN 2,000 TONS OF PAPER PER MONTH.

WITH THE AID OF INK-JET MAILING LINES, WHICH PLACE MAIL ADDRESSES DIRECTLY ON MAGAZINES, PUBLISHERS PRINTING COMPANY MAILS MORE THAN 800,000 PIECES DAILY.

John went on to become an outstanding figure in American industry; his invention and subsequent manufacture of a system for creating raw water ice made his company very successful, and by the end of the 19th century, 95 percent of all new ice plants in the country used his system.

Frank X. stayed with the printing company, bringing in his son, Alfred, to join the company in 1910. As the printing company progressed, it was known by several different names and continued to print German-oriented publications. The advent of World War I altered this course, and in 1922 the company changed its name, at Alfred's urging, to Publishers Printing Company.

In the 1940s, Alfred's son Frank E. Simon joined the company and later advanced to the position of president. Under his guidance and vision Publishers became one of Kentucky's leading printers. In 1958, Publishers relocated to Shepherdsville, and from that facility it continues its dedication to quality and service.

Publishers' Commitment to the Golden Rule

Frank E. Simon ensured that the company worked closely with publishers, editors, and their production departments to suggest how projects could best be accomplished. He relentlessly pursued the goal of finding and training superior craftspeople to carry on the living tradition of printing excellence. And, he insisted on always conducting business according to the Golden Rule: Do unto others as you would have them do unto you.

Today, his sons, Nicholas and Michael, continue his vision. "One of the major benefits to working with us," says Michael Simon, "is the fact that we're a relatively large operation, which enables us to keep up with technology, yet customers can still call up an owner here to discuss issues and ideas. If I could leave customers with one main impression of us, it would be that our honesty and integrity are foremost in our decision making, whether it concerns employees, customers, or suppliers."

THIS WEB PRESS AT PUBLISHERS PRINTING COMPANY RUNS SIGNATURES AT SPEEDS OF MORE THAN 400 FEET PER SECOND (TOP).

THE DIGITAL PREPRESS DEPARTMENT CONVERTS CUSTOMERS' ORIGINAL PHOTOS AND SLIDES INTO DIGITAL DATA IN PREPARATION FOR THE PRINTING PROCESS. MORE THAN $1 MILLION HAS BEEN INVESTED IN THIS AREA ALONE IN THE PAST YEAR (BOTTOM).

*W*HEN GEORGE GARVIN BROWN, A YOUNG PHARMACEUTICAL salesman, entered the distillery business in 1870, little did he know that he would revolutionize the industry. It was customary for purchasers of bourbon whiskey to bring their own bottles or jugs to stores, filling them up straight from the barrels. Unfortunately, maintaining product quality became a problem as unscrupulous

BROWN-FORMAN HAS GROWN TO BECOME ONE OF THE NATION'S LEADING PRODUCERS AND MARKETERS OF FINE-QUALITY CONSUMER PRODUCTS (RIGHT).

FROM ITS CORPORATE HEADQUARTERS IN LOUISVILLE, BROWN-FORMAN IS UNDER THE DIRECTION OF CHAIRMAN AND CEO OWSLEY BROWN II (BELOW).

merchants would cut the whiskey with water.

Brown solved this problem when he became the first person to bottle and seal Kentucky bourbon on-site at the distillery to assure its quality. Brown's Old Forester Kentucky Straight Bourbon Whisky thus became America's first bottled bourbon, and the flagship brand of his company. To this day, many consider Old Forester to be the best bourbon on the market.

Brown-Forman has grown to become one of the nation's leading producers of fine-quality consumer products with annual sales of $1.7 billion. Under the direction of Owsley Brown II, chairman and CEO, Brown-Forman produces and markets many of the best-known and best-loved wines and spirits in the world. They include Jack Daniel's, Canadian Mist, Southern Comfort, Early Times, Korbel champagnes, and Fetzer and Bolla wines.

But Brown-Forman's top-quality products extend beyond wines and spirits. In 1983 Lenox, Inc., the country's leading manufacturer of china and crystal products, became part of the Brown-Forman

family of companies, bringing with it Hartmann luggage. In 1991 Brown-Forman acquired Dansk International Designs—known for its contemporary tabletop products, many of which feature Scandinavian designs—and Gorhman, maker of fine silver, crystal, and china.

A Commitment to Responsibility

Brown-Forman is a firm believer in the enjoyment of wine and spirits exercised as a legal right today by more than 100 million Americans. However, the company has always been concerned about the dangers of irresponsible and illegal drinking and the problems caused by the small percentage of drinkers who misuse these products. As a founder of the Distilled Spirits Council of the United States (DISCUS), Brown-Forman has for many years underwritten public education programs on responsible drinking and has funded ongoing research on the causes of alcoholism and alcohol abuse.

Brown-Forman is also a founding member of the Century Council, a national nonprofit organization created in 1991 by concerned distillers, vintners, and brewers. The Century Council's objective is to

combat alcohol abuse and misuse, with the founding companies initially committing $65 million toward that goal. The council's priorities include reducing drunk driving and underage drinking.

Each year Brown-Forman also contributes millions of dollars to community service activities, such as the Adopt-a-Neighborhood program, affordable housing/historic renovation projects, United Way, and Fund for the Arts. In fact, in 1995 Brown-Forman contributed more than $550,000 to the latter two organizations' local fund-raising drives, placing it among the leading companies in Louisville.

Brown-Forman's commitment to excellence extends to both its business and community activities. It is supported in these efforts by its dedicated and hardworking employees.

*N*EW YORK HAS THE EMPIRE STATE BUILDING; SAN Francisco, the Golden Gate Bridge; and Paris, the Eiffel Tower. Major cities worldwide are instantly identifiable by particular structures. This is also true of Louisville and the Twin Spires of Churchill Downs. ◆ In 1995 Churchill Downs marked the 100th anniversary of the Twin Spires, which

have become a symbol of America's greatest horse race, the Kentucky Derby, and of Louisville itself. The Kentucky Derby stands as the oldest consecutively held Thoroughbred race in America.

Run for the Roses

The Derby, also known as the Run for the Roses, has become an international event. First held in 1875 before a crowd of 10,000, the event now attracts more than 130,000 spectators annually, with millions more around the world watching on television. The Derby has made legends of horses such as Triple Crown winners Whirlaway, Count Fleet, Secretariat, and Affirmed.

The Kentucky Derby Festival—two weeks of parades, fireworks, and other events leading up to the famed Run for the Roses—draws involvement from the entire community and has become a tourist attraction that rivals the Mardi Gras festival in New Orleans.

Churchill Downs has also hosted several Breeders' Cup events, including the 1994 race day, which was seen by a record crowd of 71,671.

A Rich History

The beginning of this prestigious event for three-year-old Thoroughbreds dates back to 1872, when Colonel Meriwether Lewis Clark, a prominent Louisvillian, traveled to England and France to study the format and rules for racing. Founded by Clark in 1874 as the Louisville Jockey Club, the track was developed as a means of showcasing

Kentucky's Thoroughbred breeding industry. Clark organized a group of local businessmen to provide financial backing for the track.

Under the leadership of Matt Winn, who brought a strong promotional flair to the business of racing, Churchill Downs showed its first profit in 1903, 28 years after opening. Under Winn's direction, the track became a major force in the racing industry.

In 1918 management formed the Kentucky Jockey Club, which was incorporated in 1919 as a holding company for the Louisville track and three others in Kentucky. The group became known as the American Turf Association in 1928. By 1942 the track had ended its affiliation with the association and incorporated as Churchill Downs, a name that had appeared in a local newspaper article many years before.

Racing toward the Future

Under the current administration headed by Chairman of the Board William Farish and President and CEO Tom Meeker, Churchill Downs has prospered and continues to provide the highest caliber of racing.

A key to the organization's future is the track's potential for expansion. As part of its most aggressive development effort since the days of the American Turf Association, Churchill Downs opened Hoosier Park in September 1994. The dual harness and Thoroughbred track—located in Anderson, Indiana—serves as Indiana's first pari-mutuel racetrack and Churchill Downs' first out-of-state racing site since 1937.

In addition, the company has successfully opened the Sports Spectrum, an off-season intertrack wagering facility, on Poplar Level Road in Louisville. These and other progressive developments will help Churchill Downs build on its rich history and maintain its role as a national leader in Thoroughbred racing.

THE FAMED TWIN SPIRES OF CHURCHILL DOWNS (TOP) HAVE OVERSEEN 100 YEARS OF THOROUGHBRED RACING, TAKING THE SPORT INTO THE FUTURE WITH THE SPORTS SPECTRUM, AN OFF-SITE INTERTRACK WAGERING FACILITY (BOTTOM).

THE KROGER COMPANY IS THE LARGEST FOOD RETAILER IN the United States with more than 1,200 stores. It was founded in 1883 by Barney H. Kroger in Cincinnati, Ohio. In 1995 Kroger served more people in Louisville than all of the city's other supermarkets combined and is known as the store that is "always on the cutting edge." Kroger operates more than 30 state-of-the-art combination food stores in Louisville.

"You don't get to be number one and stay number one if you don't offer the people that shop with you what they're looking for every day," says John Hackett, president of Kroger's Louisville marketing area. "The other part of the equation is being involved in the community and giving back to those that have supported you."

A Rich Heritage and Deep Roots in Louisville

Carrying its slogan of "The Cutting Edge" beyond the doors of its stores, the company takes part in myriad community and charitable activities every year, putting Kroger in the position it thrives on: playing a major role in Louisville's forward movement into the next century and beyond.

The employees of Kroger give thousands of hours each year raising money for local charities. Their hard work has paid off—Kroger has been the number one corporate contributor to the Muscular Dystrophy Campaign each year for the last several years. The company has also been recognized as the number one fund-raiser for the Children's Crusade. Kroger employees work hard for these and other great causes using an incredible array of fund-raising techniques, from car washes and bake sales to bowl-a-ramas, cookouts, sweepstakes, and many more.

Kroger is also involved in the support of Operation Brightside, Dare to Care (a food distribution program to help the needy), the Urban League, the Louisville Zoo, the Kentucky Derby Festival, Wednesday's Child, and the "SafePlace" program. Kroger's involvement in Louisville goes far beyond cash registers, produce, and shelves of groceries. Kroger goes to the heart of the community.

Committed to Supporting the Kentucky Derby

For Kroger, Derby involvement starts long before the race—it begins with the annual sponsoring of the Kentucky Derby Festival and its opening ceremonies "Thunder over Louisville," which is attended by 600,000 people each year along the banks of the Ohio River. Kroger also produces the theme song for the Kentucky Derby Festival.

Additionally, Kroger enters a hot-air balloon in the race that has become a popular fixture during

THE PROTOTYPE OF KROGER'S "FUTUREMARKET," DESIGNED TO CARRY THE COMPANY INTO THE NEXT CENTURY, WAS OPENED IN NEW ALBANY, INDIANA (RIGHT).

THE OAKS GARLAND IS AWARDED TO THE WINNING HORSE OF THE KENTUCKY OAKS RACE AND IS LOVINGLY DESIGNED BY KROGER FLORAL DESIGNERS EACH YEAR (BELOW).

Derby week. As the week rolls on, Kroger is represented in the colorful Pegasus Parade with an entry manned by employees that features "Alex," Kroger's famous meat cutter. Kroger is the number one seller of Pegasus pins, which is the major fund-raiser for the Festival itself each year. In 1994, for example, Kroger provided $252,000 to the festival through the sale of these pins. The company makes no profit from the pins and sells them as a community service.

In 1987 Kroger Floral was honored by Churchill Downs when it was selected to supply the famous Garland of Roses for the winner of the Kentucky Derby. That year Alysheba won the Derby and Kroger became a part of tradition. The 1995 race—the 121st Kentucky Derby—marked the 9th year that the Garland has been crafted by Kroger floral designers. Additionally, Churchill Downs recently asked Kroger to create a garland each year for the prestigious Kentucky Oaks, run the day before

the Derby. As the Run for the Roses has become synonymous with the Kentucky Derby, so has the Run for the Lilies with the Kentucky Oaks.

Leading Supermarkets into the Next Century

Inside its stores, Kroger is not waiting for the year 2000. As far as the company is concerned, the next century is here right now and alive in its "FutureMarkets."

Kroger has always led the way in store design, variety, selection, and price in the market. The latest design introduced to Louisville has been Kroger's FutureMarket, intended to carry customers into the next century. This unique design will spread throughout the city and the state of Kentucky. These are all-purpose, one-stop, complete stores catering to practically every taste and need of any family. The FutureMarket is easily recognizable from the moment one walks through the door, thanks mainly to its contemporary decor, neon, and

combination farmer's markets and warehouse-store look. The stores create a futuristic feeling.

Kroger's Full-Service Shoppes include full-service pharmacies, floral shops that feature worldwide delivery, nutrition departments, salad bars, fresh pastry shops, New York-style delis, cheese shops, fresh seafood shops offering both employee service and self-serve, "Custom Cut" meat shops, custom pizza shops, "European Crusty Breads" shops, farmer's market-style produce, card and party supply shops, health and beauty warehouse-style departments, book and magazine departments, film and video departments that offer both sales and rentals, "Super Savings Centers" for best deals, financial centers, and a Customer Service center, all in addition to Kroger's huge selection of general merchandise.

As Kroger moves to the FutureMarket concept, however, it will not forget what got it to the top in the first place—low prices.

KROGER IS ONE OF THE MAIN SPONSORS AND THE CREATOR OF THE DRAMATIC OPENING CEREMONIES OF THE DERBY FESTIVAL, "THUNDER OVER LOUISVILLE," WHICH IS ATTENDED ANNUALLY BY APPROXIMATELY 600,000 LOUISVILLIANS.

*T*HE ROOTS OF FOUR HOSPITALS INTERTWINED OVER A 20-YEAR period to form what is now the Alliant® Health System: Norton Hospital; Children's Hospital and Kosair Crippled Children Hospital, which consolidated in 1981 to form Kosair Children's Hospital; and Methodist Evangelical Hospital, which is known today as Alliant Medical Pavilion. Together, these hospitals have 972 licensed beds in Louisville's

FOR MORE THAN A CENTURY, NORTON HOSPITAL HAS DELIVERED QUALITY HEALTH CARE TO THE PEOPLE OF LOUISVILLE AND THE REGION (RIGHT).

LED BY AN INNOVATIVE MEDICAL STAFF, ALLIANT® HEALTH SYSTEM HOSPITALS CONSISTENTLY STRIVE TO BE ON THE LEADING EDGE OF SURGICAL PRACTICE AND TECHNOLOGY, INCLUDING A FULL RANGE OF MINIMALLY INVASIVE PROCEDURES. MANY OF THE PHYSICIANS AND SURGEONS WHO SERVE ON ALLIANT'S ADULT SERVICES AND KOSAIR CHILDREN'S HOSPITAL MEDICAL STAFFS ARE AFFILIATED WITH THE INTERNATIONALLY RECOGNIZED UNIVERSITY OF LOUISVILLE SCHOOL OF MEDICINE (BELOW).

downtown medical center, providing the highest level of inpatient care, as well as comprehensive outpatient services, to patients from 60 Kentucky and southern Indiana counties, as well as referrals from far beyond this region.

The organization serves the community through an extensive network of modern facilities, advanced medical technology, and health services to many thousands of people—not just in its Louisville hospitals, but also on the job and in neighborhood Immediate Care Centers and medical centers. In addition, Alliant Management Services, a subsidiary of Alliant, is one of the nation's largest hospital management companies with 22 community and rural facilities under contract management in Kentucky, Indiana, and Illinois.

Alliant Health System, a not-for-profit organization, is guided by

a board of directors consisting of community leaders. The not-for-profit designation means the organization has a special status granted by the community to certain organizations whose main purpose is not to generate income, but to provide for the common good.

Alliant's three Louisville medical campus facilities—Norton Hospital, Kosair Children's Hospital, and Alliant Medical Pavilion— were all created from philanthropic and/or church-affiliated organizations whose sole motivation was providing for the sick and injured. The history of each hospital is a remarkable story of dedication, resourcefulness, and compassion on the part of the founding groups.

Norton Hospital

Norton Hospital opened its doors in 1886 as Louisville's first self-supporting hospital and the first of its kind below the Mason-Dixon Line. The hospital in-

cluded one of the nation's first schools of nursing, and its medical staff was among the most distinguished in the city, including one of the early presidents of the American Medical Society.

Norton established the first recovery room, the first intensive care unit, the first artificial kidney unit, the first psychiatric unit, the first air-conditioned operating and patient rooms, the first postoperative cancer chemotherapy, and even the first adjustable hospital beds.

The hospital first became affiliated with the University of Louisville School of Medicine in the 1940s, a relationship that continues today because Norton Hospital is a tertiary-care teaching hospital.

The Women's Pavilion℠ of The Norton Hospital provides general and high-risk obstetrical care, gynecological surgery, assisted reproduction, reproductive testing, and cosmetic surgery programs. The

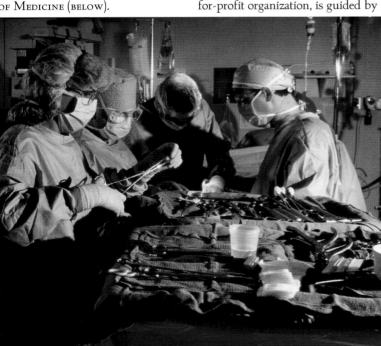

Norton Hospital Cancer Treatment Center provides comprehensive services, including gynecological, medical, and surgical oncology as well as the area's only Oncology Intensive Care Unit.

The Norton Hospital Spine and Neuroscience Center, which includes the Norton Brain Institute and the internationally recognized Kenton D. Leatherman Spine Center, is known for pioneering procedures and techniques in both spine and neurosurgery. The Norton Psychiatric Clinic is regarded internationally for its work in cognitive therapy and the treatment of adolescents, geriatric patients, alcoholism, eating disorders, and depression. Cardiovascular services range from bypass surgery to noninvasive procedures, including balloon angioplasty, rotational atherectomy, and coronary artery stents.

Kosair Children's Hospital

The only full-service children's hospital in the region, Kosair Children's Hospital is nationally recognized for its quality and level of care.

After the devastation of an 1890 tornado, which killed 75 people and injured more than 200, community concern about the state of medical care for children was galvanized. Mary Lafon organized the Hospital Circle in her church, Warren Memorial Presbyterian, the day after the storm, and officially founded the regional children's hospital. The founders garnered a broad base of community support, including financial pledges and a volunteer physician staff.

In 1892 in a converted home, Children's Free Hospital opened 25 beds to the children of Kentucky, pledging to serve "any sick or injured child sent to it who could be accommodated."

In the 1920s the Kosair Charities Committee of the Kosair Shrine Temple decided to establish an institution to fill the gap in Kentucky's health care. The founders aimed "to bring together all agencies interested in crippled children and focus the attention of the public to the wonderful possibilities in reconstruction work among children who need this

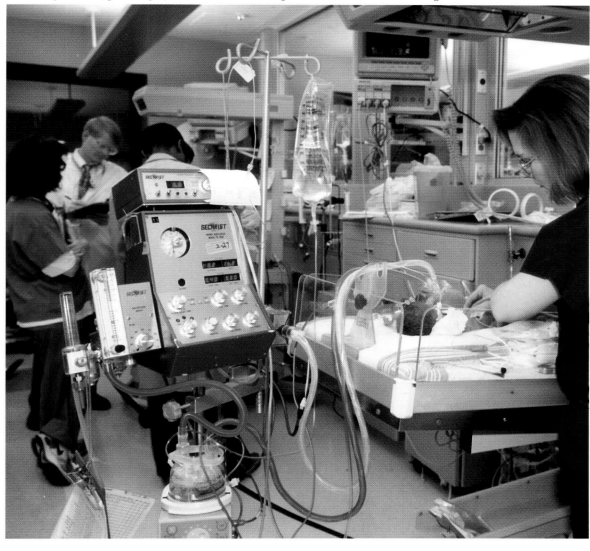

THE NEONATAL INTENSIVE CARE UNIT (NICU) AT KOSAIR CHILDREN'S HOSPITAL, AS WITH OTHER AREAS OF THIS CHILDREN'S HOSPITAL, COMBINES HIGH-TECH FACILITIES WITH A HIGH-TOUCH ENVIRONMENT. THE HOSPITAL'S NICU IS THE LIFELINE FOR MANY BABIES BORN PREMATURELY OR WITH SEVERE ILLNESSES. ANN HARRIS, R.N. (RIGHT), A NURSE IN KOSAIR CHILDREN'S HOSPITAL'S NICU, MONITORS THE PROGRESS OF A PREMATURE BABY (LEFT).

service." Kosair Crippled Children Hospital opened in 1926 and soon became recognized for its treatment of children with crippling orthopedic disorders.

After a careful look at the future, Kosair decided to mesh its special expertise with that of Children's Hospital, and the two were consolidated in 1981. The tertiary-care facility serves as the primary pediatric teaching hospital for the University of Louisville School of Medicine and serves as the region's only Trauma Center exclusively for children.

The hospital provides a full range of medical and surgical pediatric care, including the region's only pediatric burn unit; nationally recognized cancer treatment programs; neonatal and pediatric intensive care; infant/pediatric heart, kidney, liver, and bone marrow transplant programs; pediatric critical care transport services; special units for oncology, orthopedics, diabetes, psychiatry, and pediatric surgery; and the Kentucky Regional Poison Center and Office of Child Advocacy.

Kosair Children's Hospital is among the nation's top rated. The

November 1993 issue of *Child* magazine listed Kosair Children's Hospital as one of "The 10 Best Children's Hospitals in America." The 10 best hospitals were chosen from a total of 121 such facilities nationwide.

Alliant Medical Pavilion

The result of a shared mission of the United Methodist Church and the United Church of Christ, Methodist Evangelical Hospital— now Alliant Medical Pavilion— opened in 1960.

Opening with 25 patients preregistered for admission on the first day, the hospital was fondly known as "the Hilton on Broadway," boasting such high-tech touches as electric beds, central air-conditioning, push-button nurse call lights, and a hospitalwide intercom system.

Over the years the hospital expanded from 130 beds to 300. In 1972 an eight-foot replica of a surgeon's scalpel broke ground for a 64-bed east wing, housing medical/surgical beds, intensive and coronary care units, a new laboratory, emergency room, respiratory therapy department, admitting area, and business offices. In the 1980s

the hospital opened the nation's second decontamination unit, a special area designed to treat victims exposed to hazardous materials.

The Alliant Medical Pavilion is an outpatient facility and acute care medical and surgical hospital, and has 24-hour physician coverage in its Emergency Department. Centers of excellence and physician specialization include family medicine, internal medicine, oncology, ophthalmology, general orthopedics (including joint replacement and reconstruction), an arthritis treatment program, rehabilitation center, and urology.

The Diabetes and Endocrine Center, the Center for Bone and Joint Disorders, and the Decontamination Center are also located in the Alliant Medical Pavilion.

The Women's Pavilion[SM] Health & Resource Center includes the Breast Center, the Midlife Center, and the Fertility Center. Health at Work provides prevention, education, and treatment to employees of 1,500 Louisville-area companies.

Through the Alliant Health System, the Louisville area has a long-standing partner in health care.

ELIZABETH A. AMIN, M.D., RADIOLOGIST AT THE WOMEN'S PAVILION BREAST CENTER, ADJUSTS THE BIOPSY NEEDLE IN PREPARATION FOR A STEREOTACTIC BREAST BIOPSY PROCEDURE, WHICH PROVIDES THE OPTION FOR CERTAIN TYPES OF MAMMOGRAPHIC ABNORMALITIES TO BE DIAGNOSED WITHOUT SURGERY (BELOW LEFT).

ALLIANT HOSPITALS' LABORATORIES PERFORM A MYRIAD OF TESTS IN STATE-OF-THE-ART FACILITIES. MICHAEL EISENBACK, TIASCPI— AN EMPLOYEE IN KOSAIR CHILDREN'S HOSPITAL'S PATHOLOGY LAB— IS SHOWN HERE PREPARING A SOLUTION FOR ONE OF THOSE TESTS (BELOW RIGHT).

▲ D. BARTHOLOMEW

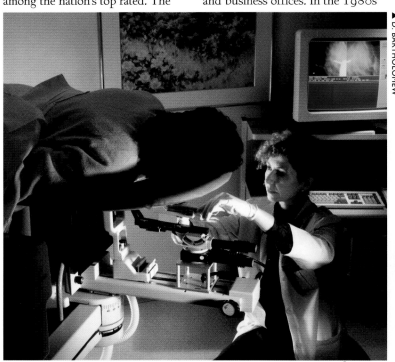

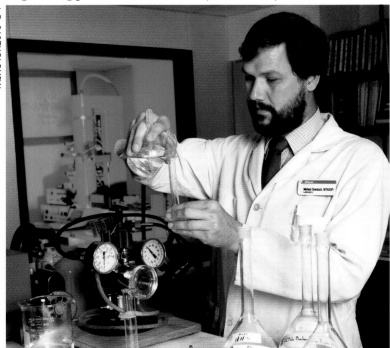

MEETING THE NEEDS OF THE COMMUNITY IT SERVES IS the focus of Spalding University. This small, urban institution offers worldwide service opportunities for students, modern training facilities for local and regional businesses, and quality education for learners of any age. ◆ Located in downtown Louisville, Spalding is an independent coeducational, Catholic university, providing both undergraduate and graduate studies for more than 1,300 students. The oldest Catholic school west of the Alleghenies, Spalding traces its educational mission to 1814 when the Sisters of Charity of Nazareth founded Nazareth Academy near Bardstown, Kentucky. College-level activity was part of the academy's program from that period.

In 1920 Nazareth College was opened in Louisville, the first four-year Catholic college for women in the commonwealth. In 1961 the college was renamed to honor Catherine Spalding, s.c.n., the founder of the Sisters of Charity of Nazareth. Although it is now owned and operated by an independent board of trustees, the school's mission and programs remain firmly rooted in ethical values and community service.

A Mission of Service at Home and Abroad

"Service is what makes us unique. It's woven into every one of our academic programs," says Dr. Thomas R. Oates, the school's president. As an example, he mentioned Spalding's international programs. "They're not your typical study abroad programs. We have social work, education, and nursing majors traveling to Ireland to work and study with Irish citizens. And students from Presentation Academy [operated by the university] are studying rain forest preservation in Belize. Students actually make a difference in these communities."

Closer to home, Spalding's emphasis on service is just as apparent. For example, Spalding was the first institution in Kentucky to offer a bachelor's degree in nursing. It is the only school in the Louisville area to offer bachelor's degrees in service professions such as social work and occupational therapy, as well as doctorates in leadership education and clinical psychology.

Meeting a Diversity of Needs

While still committed to its original core values, Spalding has grown through the years by reaching out in new ways to meet the varied needs of a diverse community. The university was instrumental in the development of the South of Broadway Business Association, a nonprofit organization that encourages growth and cooperation among businesses, schools, churches, and other organizations in the neighborhood around Spalding's campus.

Spalding has also expanded to serve the needs of Louisville's adult and business communities. Its Weekend College program lets students earn degrees entirely through weekend course work. Classes do not meet every weekend, nor are they full-day classes, yet students can still earn their degree in four years or less. In 1994 Spalding opened the Egan Leadership Center, which is used by businesses for computer training and leadership development seminars. To further serve its neighborhood and the city, Spalding University helped save Louisville's oldest continually operating school, Presentation Academy, from closing. The 1995 merger with this adjacent Catholic secondary school for girls mutually benefits both institutions and the Louisville community.

▼ EMILY WHALIN

A Magnet of Excellence

Of course, the most important aspect of Spalding's mission is to serve the needs of its own student body. With a faculty-student ratio of 1 to 16, Spalding's students are guaranteed personal attention.

More than 90 percent of full-time undergraduates also receive financial aid. As Oates says, "We want to serve diverse populations by becoming a magnet of excellence for students from all social and racial backgrounds. Spalding will find ways to provide this education for students who can't afford it."

Spalding University continues to enrich the Louisville community through its outstanding academic programs. Whether creating new opportunities for its students or working to provide special programs for the community, Spalding's emphasis on service will always be a trademark of excellence.

▼ JONATHAN ROBERTS

STUDENTS FIND THE COURTYARD OF SPALDING UNIVERSITY'S ADMINISTRATION BUILDING A FAVORITE STUDY AND RELAXATION AREA (TOP).

MEN'S AND WOMEN'S SOCCER AND BASKETBALL, AND WOMEN'S VOLLEYBALL ARE THE INTERCOLLEGIATE SPORTS PROGRAMS OFFERED AT SPALDING UNIVERSITY.

*A*NYONE FAMILIAR WITH THE LEGAL PROFESSION KNOWS that the bulk of work performed by attorneys doesn't involve actual trial activity. In fact, many lawyers never even appear in court. But the Louisville firm of Boehl Stopher & Graves can boast that 90 percent of its attorneys actively try cases in civil court. ◆ Founded in Louisville in 1895 as

▼ TED WATHEN / QUADRANT

IN ADDITION TO ITS LOUISVILLE LOCATION (RIGHT), BOEHL STOPHER & GRAVES HAS OFFICES IN LEXINGTON, PADUCAH, AND PRESTONSBURG, KENTUCKY, AS WELL AS IN NEW ALBANY, INDIANA.

BOEHL STOPHER & GRAVES IS ONE OF THE FIVE LARGEST LAW FIRMS IN THE LOUISVILLE AREA WITH A STAFF OF SOME 70 ATTORNEYS ASSISTED BY MORE THAN TWO DOZEN PARALEGALS, AS WELL AS RESEARCHERS AND OTHER STAFF WITH SPECIFIC AREAS OF EXPERTISE (BELOW).

Blakey, Quinn & Lewis, the firm has a century of experience in civil trial work. Although it has changed names four times since then, Boehl Stopher & Graves has never merged with another firm in its history.

"We're somewhat unique in that respect," says Edward H. Stopher, one of the firm's general partners. "All of our growth has been internal. That has allowed us to stay focused on what we do best—civil litigation."

The firm is managed today by a three-person executive committee composed of Stopher, Larry L. Johnson, and William O. Guethlein. While there is always a lead attorney for each case, the partners believe strongly in fostering a team atmosphere, with other attorneys, researchers, and paralegal staff available to assist with any case.

Landmarks in Civil Court Defense

While Boehl Stopher & Graves is engaged in the general practice of law, its experience with civil trial work has affected the type of work the firm most often handles. Typical cases include product liability, antitrust, aviation litigation, contract law, corporate law, estate planning and administration, labor law, negligence, admiralty law, and securities litigation.

In its history, the firm has successfully defended several major corporations in high-profile jury trials. These clients include CSX Transportation, Inc.; AlliedSignal, Inc.; Eli Lilly and Company; Ford Motor Company; Texas Eastern Transmission Company; and Champion International, Inc. The firm successfully defended several workers' compensation cases resulting in landmark decisions, which eventually led to changes in laws regulating payments to claimants.

◀ TED WATHEN / QUADRANT

The firm's efforts have earned numerous awards and other recognition. For nearly 40 years, Boehl Stopher & Graves has carried an AV rating—the highest available—in the nationally published *Martindale Hubbell Law Directory.* Six of the firm's active attorneys have been named to the Best Lawyers in America, and three of the active attorneys have been elected to the American College of Trial Lawyers.

Evolving to Handle a Larger Caseload

Boehl Stopher & Graves is one of the five largest legal practices in the Louisville area. It was the first law firm in Kentucky to open a satellite office when it expanded its services to Lexington more than 45 years ago. In addition to the Lexington location, the firm now has offices in Paducah and Prestonsburg, Kentucky, as well as in New Albany, Indiana.

Most of the firm's growth has occurred recently. Today Boehl Stopher & Graves has a staff of about 70 attorneys, which is nearly seven times the number it employed 25 years ago. These attorneys are assisted by more than two dozen paralegals, as well as researchers and other staff with specific areas of expertise.

Stopher points to two primary reasons for the firm's growth. One is the increase in the volume of product liability and medical malpractice suits. The other is the firm's ability to take advantage of new technology and trial preparation techniques to successfully carry the increased volume of cases to resolution.

Boehl Stopher & Graves utilizes a state-of-the-art computer system that streamlines legal research, document retrieval, and billing procedures. Computers are used extensively to help prepare exhibits and organize documents for each case. In addition, the firm's team approach allows much of the case preparation work to be handled by paralegals

▲ JOHN BECKMAN / QUADRANT

and other support staff, so clients can get top-notch trial representation without unnecessary expense.

Along with their involvement in civil court defense, many employees are also active with nonprofit, community-oriented causes, including educational, civic, charitable, and religious organizations. Boehl Stopher & Graves remains committed to Louisville as its home base. That was one of the reasons the partners recently chose to relocate the firm's offices to the 22nd and 23rd

floors of Providian Center, Kentucky's tallest building.

"Our founders were from Louisville. We've been here for nearly 100 years and have grown with the community," maintains Stopher.

Looking ahead, Stopher says that while the firm should continue to expand, the partners do not plan to stray from the original mission of the organization. "We are prepared and ready to see a case through to a resolution," he adds, "either through mediation, arbitration, or jury trial."

BOEHL STOPHER & GRAVES REMAINS COMMITTED TO LOUISVILLE AS ITS HOME BASE AND RECENTLY RELOCATED THE FIRM'S OFFICES TO THE 22ND AND 23RD FLOORS OF PROVIDIAN CENTER, KENTUCKY'S TALLEST BUILDING (ABOVE).

THE SEELBACH HOTEL

T HE SEELBACH HOTEL, A MASTERWORK OF TURN-of-the-century elegance in atmosphere and decor, was first opened in 1905 by brothers Louis and Otto Seelbach. Today, The Seelbach maintains its status among the elite hotels of the world. The hotel has been recognized by James Tackach in his book *Great American Hotels: Luxury Palaces and Elegant Resorts*, and it

is listed on the National Register of Historic Places. The Seelbach takes pride in carrying on the grand traditions of times past, blending elegance in decor with modern, sophisticated service.

Historical Past Enriches the Present

The Seelbach's beginnings predate its actual opening, starting when Louis and Otto Seelbach immigrated to Louisville from Germany in 1869 and 1878, respectively. Louis, only 17 when he came to America, learned the hotel business by working for one of Louisville's prominent hotels. In the American tradition, he went out on his own and, in 1874, opened Seelbach's Restaurant and Cafe, which quickly won a devoted following.

In 1880, building on its reputa-tion for the best dining in the city, Louis moved the restaurant to larger quarters. Six years later, the brothers reunited to form The Seelbach Hotel Company and, in 1886, opened a 30-room hotel over the restaurant. Wishing to transform their hotel into the most beautiful in town, the brothers closed it in 1890 and spent 10 years transforming the property into a sumptuous, Euro-pean-style hotel. Upon reopening in 1900, the brothers again enjoyed immediate success.

Though the original hotel was elegant, the brothers' ultimate goal was yet to be realized—to build one of the finest hotels in the nation. In 1902 the Seelbachs began building their dream in downtown Louis-ville. Sparing no expense, the broth-ers imported marble from around the world, bronze from France, hardwood from the West Indies, linens from Ireland, special china and glassware patterns, and Oriental rugs. The lobby featured a drinking fountain made from one of the larg-est pieces of Rookwood pottery ever cast, and huge murals of pio-neer scenes painted by famed New York artist Arthur Thomas. The total cost of the new hotel was $950,000—an almost unheard-of sum for Louisville in those times.

The opening party for the new Seelbach Hotel was one of the big-gest ever seen in Louisville. More than 25,000 people toured the facility, and over 2,000 more had to be turned away in the five-hour period during which it was open for public viewing. During the official grand opening, 1,500 members of Louisville's business, social, and political elite came through the doors to dine, dance, and socialize. Continued success brought on a $300,000 addition, including 154 guest rooms, a covered ballroom off

LOCATED IN THE HEART OF DOWN-TOWN LOUISVILLE, THE SEELBACH HOTEL IS LISTED ON THE NATIONAL REGISTER OF HISTORIC PLACES (RIGHT).

THE FAMOUS SEELBACH RATHSKEL-LER IS TREASURED AS THE WORLD'S ONLY ROOKWOOD POTTERY ROOM THAT IS STILL INTACT (BELOW).

the Roof Garden, and the famous Seelbach Rathskeller with its rare Rookwood pottery decor. Today, the Rathskeller is treasured as the world's only Rookwood pottery room still intact.

Hard Times and Rebirth

Louis Seelbach died in 1925, and in 1929, Otto retired. Prohibition closed the famous and profitable Rathskeller until it reopened in 1934 under different ownership. While the hotel survived Louisville's devastating 1937 flood, The Seelbach was unable to weather the increasing costs of operating a hotel in the grand manner. Though it remained a mecca for the elite and its fame endured for decades, declining fortunes forced the hotel's closure on July 1, 1975.

Through the combined efforts of the Kentucky Heritage Commission, the Center City Commission, the City of Louisville, Metropolitan Life Insurance, actor/investor Roger Davis, and construction company president H.G. Whittenberg Jr., $17 million in financing was obtained, and the hotel was completely renovated and reopened on April 13, 1982. The Seelbach Hotel was reborn into the grandeur that its founders had dreamed of at the turn of the century. In 1983 The Seelbach became one of only 40 hotels worldwide to be selected by the prestigious Preferred Hotels Association. The Seelbach is now owned and managed by Medallion Hotels, New York.

Still an American Symbol

While The Seelbach presents a historic setting for guests, the facility also provides a full-service, state-of-the-art site for meetings, conferences, and special events. A recent expansion brings the total available meeting space to more than 32,000 square feet. The primary focus of The Seelbach's staff of 380 is to create the best possible experience for guests, whether they are visiting

for business or pleasure. Cutting-edge technology in areas from sales and catering to the latest meeting room systems is just part of the hotel's ongoing mission to automate and streamline guest services.

The Seelbach aggressively seeks innovative ways to maintain

the highest level of service in the most cost-effective manner. Increasingly sophisticated travelers with ever higher expectations continually challenge the management and staff of The Seelbach to remain ahead of the industry in service, technology, and satisfaction.

ITALIAN AND SWISS MARBLE PILLARS GREET VISITORS IN THE LOBBY OF THE SEELBACH HOTEL. THE LOBBY ALSO FEATURES ORIGINAL MURALS DEPICTING HISTORICAL EVENTS FROM PIONEER DAYS IN KENTUCKY BY RENOWNED NEW YORK PAINTER ARTHUR THOMAS.

BRANDEIS MACHINERY & SUPPLY CORPORATION

$\mathcal{S}$INCE 1908 BRANDEIS MACHINERY & SUPPLY CORPORATION has been serving the needs of local construction and mining equipment users. Over the years, the company has expanded throughout Kentucky, Indiana, and southeastern Illinois, and has become one of the largest Komatsu and Ingersoll-Rand dealers in the country. Brandeis offers total product support for a

wide range of new, used, and rental equipment.

"Brandeis is associated with the most respected manufacturers of heavy, general, and light equipment," says President and COO Gene Snowden. "We provide our customers with comprehensive machine-to-job matching capabilities, whatever the application."

Brandeis' thorough knowledge of its customers, their needs, and their business challenges has distinguished the company since its inception. Founded by Robert E. Brandeis, the original business occupied a 2,000-square-foot building and had two employees. Focused on supplying equipment to the turn-of-the-century construction industry in Louisville, Brandeis saw that his company would grow as the city prospered, and that industrial growth was soon to follow.

THROUGH ITS ASSOCIATION WITH WELL-KNOWN MANUFACTURERS, BRANDEIS HAS GROWN TO BECOME A COMPREHENSIVE SOURCE OF NEW, USED, AND LONG-TERM RENTAL EQUIPMENT (RIGHT).

THE NEARLY 200 EMPLOYEES AT BRANDEIS FOCUS ON THREE MAIN AREAS: SELLING AND RENTING NEW AND USED EQUIPMENT; SELLING SPECIFIC MANUFACTURER AND GENERIC PARTS; AND PERFORMING SERVICE WORK (BELOW).

After Brandeis' death in 1924, another Louisvillian, J.A. Paradis Sr., became president and owner of the company, followed by his son J.A. Paradis Jr. Now his grandson J.A. Paradis III continues to lead the company in line with the founder's vision.

Brandeis Machinery & Supply Corporation is a subsidiary of Bramco, Inc. and a sister company of RESCO RENTS (Rental Equipment Service Company). As the oldest and largest member of the Bramco organization, Brandeis focuses on three main areas: selling and renting new and used equipment; selling specific manufacturer and generic parts; and performing service work. The company's 122,000-square-foot headquarters is located in eastern Jefferson County and employs more than 200 people in facilities located in Louisville, Lexington, Corbin, and Stanville, Kentucky, and in Indianapolis, Fort Wayne, and Evansville, Indiana.

Strong Customer Focus

The company's success is the result of its ability to develop and maintain strong customer relationships. Brandeis has led the industry in customer-driven innovation because its number-one focus is to satisfy its customers' needs.

The company adheres to the principles of total quality management (TQM), implementing a process that includes identifying and

anticipating customer needs and expectations, improving every aspect of customer service, reducing costs that result in savings for customers, and decreasing customers' overall operating costs. Brandeis' commitment to continuous improvement has been recognized through awards such as the Komatsu Excellence Chairman's Award, which Brandeis has received every year since the award's inception. In addition, Brandeis has received the Simon Ingersoll Award for six consecutive years—an award given to Ingersoll-Rand's top distributor. Brandeis is also a founding member of the Associated Equipment Distributors.

Service orientation also extends to employee relations. "Brandeis is known in the industry as a premier company with high morals and standards," says Snowden. "We treat everyone with respect and truly believe in continuous improvement of ourselves and our communities. Over the years, the company has developed a culture in which people enjoy work and feel at home. This gives us a significant advantage in our industry because we can recruit and retain the best employees."

*W*HAT STARTED AS A CONSTRUCTION EQUIPMENT DISTRI-butor in 1908 under the name of Brandeis Machinery and Supply Corporation expanded in 1966 to include RESCO RENTS (Rental Equipment Service Company), one of the largest equipment rental networks in the country. From its original office in Louisville's Bowman Field Airport, RESCO RENTS has grown to 120

employees, with 16 locations covering the eastern region of the United States.

Boasting a comprehensive line of rental construction and industrial equipment, RESCO RENTS has it all—whether customers need a single air compressor or an entire fleet of dozers. A complete array of late-model, high-quality construction equipment is available for rent by the day, week, or month. RESCO RENTS' experienced, well-trained personnel have a thorough knowledge of machine capabilities so they are able to assist customers in matching the right equipment with the right application.

"Our customers can have their entire equipment needs taken care of by us," says President and COO Steven Paradis. "In fact, we assure maximum availability of equipment through our 24-hour, seven-day-a-week service line. The entire RESCO RENTS system is designed to keep customers on schedule and on the job."

But the company's commitment to fleet efficiency goes beyond maximum availability. Each piece of equipment undergoes regular servicing and safety inspection to assure the highest level of operational reliability. The company's factory-trained service technicians maintain demanding standards to minimize the possibility of downtime. Should a breakdown occur, RESCO RENTS will immediately replace or repair the equipment on-site.

Branching Out to Serve a Variety of Needs

In 1993 RESCO RENTS launched a second division called RESCO POWER, which specializes in renting quiet-generator packages, electrical distribution systems, and light towers. RESCO POWER provides turnkey power solutions for industrial, commercial, construction, and special-event applications.

"Our mobile generators are designed to eliminate changeover, routine or emergency maintenance, and power outages. Every piece of RESCO POWER equipment is backed by unparalleled technical assistance and 24-hour service, so customers know they have reliable solutions in managing all their power requirements," Paradis notes. "Unlike some businesses that merely rent electrical generators, leaving the customer to handle setup, RESCO POWER provides customized setup to meet any power need. We take care of all the details to ensure customers receive everything they need for safe, quiet, and continuous power."

Aside from providing power to contractors and industrial clients such as the General Electric and Ford plants, one of RESCO POWER's biggest special-event customers is the city's Thunder Over Louisville fireworks extravaganza. RESCO POWER provides between 70 and 80 generators that supply all the power for this exciting Derby Festival event.

Both RESCO RENTS and RESCO POWER are dedicated to providing the highest value to their customers, top-quality equipment, and unmatched service through their courteous and professional personnel. It is this dedication to customers, believes Paradis, that will position the company for a prosperous future and a strong standing in the equipment rental industry.

BOASTING A COMPREHENSIVE LINE OF RENTAL CONSTRUCTION AND INDUSTRIAL EQUIPMENT, RESCO RENTS HAS IT ALL—WHETHER CUSTOMERS NEED A SINGLE AIR COMPRESSOR OR AN ENTIRE FLEET OF DOZERS.

F OR MORE THAN EIGHT DECADES, THE ORGANIZATION known today as Great Financial Bank has evolved to meet the financial needs of the region it serves. ◆ When three Louisville businessmen gathered in 1915 to create the Greater Louisville Savings and Building Association, the lines between thrift institutions and banks were clear, and remained so for three

generations. But by the time those lines began to blur in the early 1980s, Greater Louisville's successor, Great Financial Federal, had become Kentucky's largest mutual savings and loan, with financial strength that ranked among the nation's best.

"Great Financial has been a sound financial institution for 80 years," says Paul M. Baker, chairman and chief executive officer. "During the 1980s—a time that was troubling for many thrifts—we continued to grow and prosper. And we continue to maintain a strong financial position even in today's competitive environment."

A Future to Bank On

One of the most dramatic changes in the history of the company occurred in early 1994, when Great Financial received approval to convert to a publicly traded, federal savings bank. With the conversion, the organization was renamed Great Financial Bank, FSB and began a forward-looking transformation to a strong mortgage lending and retail banking institution with a full range of banking products and services.

Today community banking is Great Financial's focus, and it has aggressively implemented a full range of retail banking products and services, including credit cards; debit cards; and auto, equity, and other consumer loans. Great Financial intends to be a leading source of competitive financial products and services by making banking more convenient, expanding product lines, and providing superior service.

"In 1994, we unveiled our new logo, which emphasizes the

word 'bank' in bold, new corporate colors," notes Baker. "We also introduced new print and TV advertising that stresses our intention to become the most user-friendly bank in the communities we serve. Becoming more customer-focused is not just a look; it's the way we conduct our business."

Banking for the People, by the People

Several types of checking accounts enable today's Great Financial Bank customers to match features with their individual needs. They can minimize cash transactions by using two of the world's most widely accepted credit cards, as well as debit cards that provide free

access to MAC® regional automated teller machines and to the national CIRRUS® network. In addition to mortgages and construction lending, the bank's lending products include consumer loans, as well as home equity loans and lines of credit, and personal lines of credit.

Customers can build assets through three types of savings accounts and certificates of deposit, as well as through alternative investment opportunities offered by Great Financial Services. Products for personal investing and individual retirement accounts (IRAs) include brokerage services, annuities, mutual funds, and unit investment trusts (UITs). Trust services are also being expanded, and safety deposit

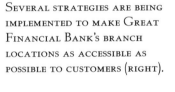

box services and small-business banking products are being offered.

With Great Financial's conversion, each of its locations is either being adapted or relocated to accommodate full-service banking functions, such as drive-in banking, ATM access, and night depository, among others. "We are implementing several strategies, such as operating branches in supermarket locations, to make our services as accessible to customers as possible," says Baker.

A Proud Part of the American Dream

Mortgage lending is the cornerstone of Great Financial, and the company is proud of its role in helping so many people fulfill their dreams—whether for the purchase of an existing residence, the construction of a new home, or the financing of a commercial venture.

"Our goal is to exceed the expectations of our customers—buyers, sellers, real estate agents, and builders—by offering quality service, competitive rates, and attractive products," explains Baker.

To make mortgage financing as simple and convenient as possible, Great Financial offers a variety of user-friendly services, including preapproved loan amounts, lender assistance on closing costs, low down payments, a wide variety of loan products, and home equity loans or lines of credit.

Programs like Great Financial's Great Beginnings loan are targeted to low- to moderate-income families and increases their ability to afford a home by providing below-market interest rates and high loan-to-value ratios without the additional cost of private mortgage insurance.

A Responsible Corporate Citizen

As the largest financial institution headquartered in Kentucky, Great Financial takes very seriously its responsibility to contribute to the quality of life in the communities it serves. All across the state, the bank and its employees donate time and money to make a difference in community organizations and activities. The involvement takes many forms.

For instance, in the area of education, Great Financial has formed a partnership with higher education in Kentucky to provide a number of annual scholarships to deserving high school and college students. Great Financial is also a strong supporter of United Way across the state, as well as efforts like Habitat for Humanity that make home ownership possible for low-income families. The company also supports a number of civic and cultural efforts that improve the lives of local citizens.

Whatever its role—whether as community bank or corporate citizen—Great Financial Bank realizes that its continued success depends on maintaining the support and trust of its customers and shareholders. "We intend never to betray that trust," says Baker, "and will continue to work in every way to reward the loyalty and confidence expressed through the investment our customers and shareholders have made in our organization."

CLOCKWISE FROM TOP RIGHT: GREAT FINANCIAL COMBINES TECHNOLOGY AND HUMAN RESOURCES TO PROVIDE INSTANT CASH ADVANCES, CAR LOANS, AND OTHER PERSONAL FINANCING.

GREAT FINANCIAL OFFERS MASTERCARD® AND VISA® CLASSIC AND GOLD CARDS TAILORED TO THE PERSONAL FINANCIAL NEEDS OF ITS CUSTOMERS.

GREAT FINANCIAL IS COMMITTED TO SERVING EACH OF ITS CUSTOMERS ON A PERSONALIZED, INDIVIDUAL BASIS.

ASHLAND INC.

ESTABLISHED IN 1924 AS A SMALL EASTERN KENTUCKY REFINERY, Ashland Inc. has grown into a worldwide energy and chemical company. With headquarters in Russell, Ashland boasts more than 32,500 employees worldwide. ◆ The company is probably best known to consumers through its 609 Super-America station/store outlets in 11 states and through the

products it markets under the Valvoline® brand, the oldest name and trademark in use in the petroleum industry.

A Welcome Sight

SuperAmerica station/stores are a welcome sight along roadways throughout the Ohio Valley and upper Midwest. In addition to high-quality fuels and quick-stop grocery items, SuperAmerica adds value for consumers by offering fresh bakery goods, automotive accessories, and easy access to automated teller machines. In a bid to further bolster its highly effective, one-stop shopping concept, SuperAmerica is adding brand-name fast foods through partnerships with Taco Bell® and Subway®.

Valvoline markets motor oils, greases, gear oils, automatic transmission fluids, and antifreeze through a network of distributors and retailers. Continuing to expand its reputation as an environmental leader and "total fluids management" company, Valvoline recently enhanced its used-oil collection service for automotive retailers and installers. In addition, Valvoline Instant Oil Change has become one of the nation's largest quick-lube chains, with more than 360 company-operated outlets in 14 states.

Ashland has remained true to its roots in refining and is one of the nation's most efficient independent refiners, with a total capacity of 354,200 barrels per day through its Ashland Petroleum division. The company also has a strategic presence in petrochemicals through its Ashland Chemical division, the

ASHLAND INC. HAS REMAINED TRUE TO ITS ROOTS IN REFINING AND IS ONE OF THE NATION'S MOST EFFICIENT INDEPENDENT REFINERS, WITH A TOTAL CAPACITY OF 354,200 BARRELS PER DAY THROUGH ITS ASHLAND PETROLEUM DIVISION (RIGHT).

ASHLAND INC.'S SUPERAMERICA STATION/STORES ARE A WELCOME SIGHT ALONG ROADWAYS THROUGHOUT THE OHIO VALLEY AND UPPER MIDWEST, OFFERING HIGH-QUALITY FUELS AND QUICK-STOP GROCERY ITEMS (BELOW).

largest North American distributor of chemicals and plastics. The Industrial Chemicals and Solvents division markets chemical products and solvents to industrial clients in major markets through a distribution network that includes a warehouse in Louisville. The firm's APAC group is the largest highway contractor in the United States.

High Profile in Louisville

As the largest city in Kentucky, Louisville has always been important to Ashland, and vice versa. The company employs more than 600 local residents and enjoys a high profile within the community through its 29 SuperAmerica station/stores and 15 Valvoline Instant Oil Change outlets.

"Louisville is special to us," says Ashland spokesperson David Sattich. "We tend to give Louisville more attention than other markets of comparable size simply because of the valuable role the city has played in the history of our company."

Ashland has made substantial contributions to area charities. The United Way, March of Dimes, and American Cancer Society all benefit from this community spirit.

Because well-educated, highly skilled employees make much of Ashland's success possible, the major thrust of the company's community activism is the promotion of high standards of excellence in education. For the Louisville area, these efforts include Ashland's Teacher Achievement Awards program, a company-sponsored Day on Campus field trip program, and longtime sponsorship of WAVE-TV's academic quiz show, "High-Q."

"The Ashland philosophy calls for its employees to become actively involved in the community," says Sattich. "We don't just work here. We live here, and that calls for quite a commitment from all of us."

DIXIE WAREHOUSE & CARTAGE CO.

DIXIE WAREHOUSE & CARTAGE CO. IS AMONG THE nation's leading providers of distribution logistics—the combined services of warehousing, transporting, and handling a customer's products—for wholesale and industrial customers. Although Dixie plays a key role in the distribution strategies of some of Louisville's most

prominent manufacturers, the company is more accurately viewed as a global service provider, shipping customers' products worldwide.

With a track record of safety and efficiency, Dixie has earned its position as the warehousing and logistics supplier of choice for Fortune 500 companies in the automotive, appliance, chemical, computer, electronics, grocery, tobacco, and manufactured raw materials industries. Dixie recently constructed Kentucky's first and only public warehouse for flammable liquid storage. This expansion establishes Dixie as a provider of unique and highly advanced facilities for regional customers who previously had to look to other parts of the country.

Family Success Story

Founded in 1938 by R. W. Rounsavall Jr., Dixie Warehouse & Cartage Co. is currently owned jointly by the founder's sons, Robert W. Rounsavall III and G. Hunt Rounsavall. Today, more than 300 employees work in Dixie's four locations—the main site in Louisville; a contract site in Schaumburg, Illinois; Dixie Technical Service in Raleigh, North Carolina; and Beaumont Distribution Service in Beaumont, Texas.

Among the factors crucial to Dixie's success are the company's energetic, creative, and progressive management team and skilled employees, all of whom are focused on serving the customer. Dixie's owners and management are dedicated to investing in the best people, the most thorough training, and the latest technology in

order to achieve cost-effective distribution solutions for its clients.

Changing to Serve Customer Needs

When Dixie started out in the late 1930s, the warehousing and distribution business was a labor-intensive process, both in the warehouse and in the office. While labor-saving devices, such as the forklift, significantly improved operations in the early years, computerization has had an even more striking effect. Today, the precise location of every case and carton in Dixie's warehouses can be pinpointed by computer. Customer orders that formerly arrived in the mail are now transmitted instantaneously from the customer's computer into Dixie's system. Manual inventories that were taken only once a year are now monitored continuously by computer.

Customer feedback has been the catalyst for change in Dixie's ability to satisfy clients' needs, revealing a fundamental shift in the way Dixie's customers think about inventory. This shift fuels ongoing improvement in the speed of service, which can be seen in the compression of the entire customer order cycle from days to minutes. Stronger emphasis is now placed on product movement, rapid inventory turns, short reaction times, and lower costs.

Community Contributor

The Rounsavall brothers are directors on the boards of Louisville charitable and business organizations. Robert W. Rounsavall III is chairman of the Kentucky Center

for the Arts. G. Hunt Rounsavall is chairman of the Alliant Hospital board. In addition, the company provides financial support to the University of Louisville, the Greater Louisville Fund for the Arts, the J. B. Speed Art Museum, and the Actors Theatre of Louisville, to name only a few. G. Hunt Rounsavall cofounded the Kentuckiana Children's House—Louisville's Ronald McDonald House—for which Dixie employees have raised more than $100,000 during the past 10 years.

By playing an active role in contributing to the Louisville community and a leading role in providing both national and international distribution logistics services to its clients, Dixie Warehouse and Cartage Co. will continue to be a corporate leader well into the next century.

FOUNDED IN 1938 BY R. W. ROUNSAVALL JR., DIXIE WAREHOUSE & CARTAGE CO. IS CURRENTLY OWNED JOINTLY BY THE FOUNDER'S SONS, ROBERT W. ROUNSAVALL III (ON RIGHT) AND G. HUNT ROUNSAVALL (TOP).

FROM ITS 1950S LOCATION AT 10TH AND MAIN STREETS, DIXIE CARTAGE SAW THE WAREHOUSING AND DISTRIBUTION BUSINESS MAKE GREAT STRIDES. TODAY, MORE THAN 300 EMPLOYEES WORK IN DIXIE'S THREE LOCATIONS (BOTTOM).

CORHART REFRACTORIES

NLY A HANDFUL OF COMPANIES IN THIS COUNTRY CAN CLAIM to be part of a 330-year-old, multinational organization. Among them are Louisville-based Corhart Refractories and Quartz Products Company, owned by Compagnie de Saint-Gobain, who, headquartered in Paris, specializes in engineered materials and is listed among the 100 largest industrial groups worldwide. Together, Corhart Refractories and Quartz Products employ 300 Louisvillians.

Perhaps one of the best-kept secrets in Louisville, Corhart has developed state-of-the-art glass-industry refractories, primarily serving customers in other parts of the United States. Its products—heat-resistant ceramic materials made in the form of bricks, large blocks, or slabs—line glass-making furnaces around the world and, by withstanding ultrahigh temperatures, help turn sand into molten glass.

Developing a Better Way
Just after World War I, the Corning Glass Works set out to develop a refractory that could withstand a continuous glass-melting operation. Researchers, noting that a material called mullite remained unmelted in glass, reasoned that this material could be used for refractories. Discovery of this material, however, was only half the solution. The other half was how mullite could be melted and formed into a refractory block without also melting the container. The solution developed by the researchers

was to electrically fuse the raw materials, using them as their own container. These Electrocast refractory blocks quickly revolutionized glass-making.

In 1927, Corning entered into a joint venture with Hartford-Empire, a company with strong ties to glass manufacturing. The new company—named Corhart—began producing, here in Louisville, the first Electrocast refractories for Corning. These first products were an immediate success and within 15 years 80 percent of the glass-making industry was using the product. This success led to the creation of the company's own research laboratory in Louisville in 1936. Following World War II, the firm developed refractories for use in the steel industry.

Over the years, the always-profitable Corhart has continued to successfully serve its markets and has excelled particularly in international sales, exporting more than one-third of its products.

The overall strength of Corhart led to its acquisition in 1987 by the Industrial Ceramics Branch of the Saint-Gobain Group of France. This makes Corhart a strategic U.S. component in one of the world's largest industrial ceramics companies.

A Visible Contributor to the Community
Corhart is also a visible contributor to the Louisville community. Principal among the firm's activities is its ongoing involvement in Junior Achievement; the company is a major benefactor to Junior Achievement and, in addition, a large number of its salaried employees serve as volunteer instructors at local schools. The company also maintains close ties to the University of Louisville's Speed Scientific School and the School of Business and Public Administration.

Corhart is well prepared to move through the 1990s and into the 21st century. The tradition of innovation and dedication to development of new and better products not only continues, but is also backed by a strong investment in research and development. In fact, 5 percent of all revenue, more than the industry standard, is directed into research and development, ensuring Corhart's commitment to preeminence in industrial ceramic technology.

OVER THE YEARS, THE ALWAYS-PROFITABLE CORHART HAS CONTINUED TO SUCCESSFULLY SERVE ITS MARKETS AND HAS EXCELLED PARTICULARLY IN INTERNATIONAL SALES, EXPORTING MORE THAN ONE-THIRD OF ITS PRODUCTS.

QUARTZ PRODUCTS COMPANY

WHEN NASA SPACE SHUTTLES BLAST INTO THE HEAVENS, they carry with them a little piece of Louisville. On board those flights is Quartzel®, a fused quartz glass fiber made by Quartz Products Company (QPC), a firm headquartered in Louisville and a worldwide leader in the industry. Because of their unique thermal and electrical properties, fused quartz fibers

are being used in an ever-increasing range of high-tech applications. In addition to being used by NASA, Quartzel is used in high-speed printed circuit boards for computers, the military's Stealth aircraft, and commercial aircraft, and in sporting goods from golf clubs to tennis rackets.

From France to Louisville

QPC, along with Corhart Refractories, is owned by the Saint-Gobain Group of France. Quartzel was developed by a QPC sister company in France during the early 1960s. QPC, then located in New Jersey, was the U. S. distributor of the French-produced yarn. QPC joined its sister company Corhart Refractories in Louisville in 1987. In 1988, responding to U.S. Department of Defense needs, QPC built a new, 50,000-square-foot factory and began production of Quartzel in Louisville (Riverport).

In addition to Quartzel, QPC produces a variety of fused quartz products at its Riverport facility. Fabricated tubing, plates, and discs made from pure fused quartz materials are provided to customer specifications and used by a variety of industries such as semiconductor manufacturers and heating systems companies. QPC also maintains a national distribution center at Riverport for shipment of a variety of products made by sister companies in the United Kingdom and France.

QPC achieved a substantial growth in sales in 1994, and continued growth is expected throughout the balance of the 90s, clearly demonstrating that it is among the world's top producers and distributors of fused quartz materials.

Building Success on Employees

Part of what's made QPC so successful is its commitment to the principle of total quality management (TQM). The company has five quality teams that address issues such as increasing employee satisfaction and improving the total customer experience. QPC devotes a large portion of its overall time to such goals, making TQM an integral part of its company values and structure. The company also encourages employee involvement in all operations and spends significant time on safety and environmental issues, as well as on increasing community involvement. Executive members of both QPC and Corhart meet quarterly, assessing artistic, educational, and community activities to which they should allocate resources. Like Corhart, many of QPC's employees are actively involved in the local Junior Achievement. QPC strives to be a good corporate citizen, and has contributed to civic, education, and health and human service activities that enhance the quality of life.

Indeed, QPC is like all the Saint-Gobain companies around the world: It focuses on strengthening its leadership position through research and development; through attention to the impact of its plant on the environment; through the quality of its products, services, investments, and management performance; and through the active participation of employees at all levels in contributing to continuous improvement.

QPC FOCUSES ON STRENGTHENING ITS LEADERSHIP POSITION THROUGH RESEARCH AND DEVELOPMENT, AND THE QUALITY OF ITS PRODUCTS, SERVICES, INVESTMENTS, AND MANAGEMENT PERFORMANCE.

*M*ANY COMPANIES ARE JUSTIFIABLY PROUD TO CELEBRATE 25, 50, even 100 years in business. In 1994, Devoe & Raynolds celebrated its 240th birthday. Not surprisingly, that makes Devoe & Raynolds the oldest paint maker in the country. But Devoe is also recognized as the oldest company of any kind in Louisville, and the ninth-oldest company of any

THE COMPANY NOW KNOWN AS DEVOE & RAYNOLDS BEGAN IN 1754 WHEN WILLIAM POST OPENED A STORE ON WATER STREET IN NEW YORK CITY TO SELL HIS OWN GROUND PIGMENTS (BELOW). WITH FACILITIES IN LOUISVILLE SINCE 1928, DEVOE'S INNOVATIVE, QUALITY PRODUCTS HAVE MADE IT ONE OF THE TOP 10 PAINT AND COATINGS MANUFACTURERS IN THE UNITED STATES (BOTTOM).

kind in the United States.

Thanks to an ongoing commitment to innovation, Devoe is one of the top 10 paint and coatings manufacturers in the United States. Located in Louisville since 1928, Devoe sells a complete line of paints under its Devoe Paint label to commercial, professional contractor, and home users. Devoe Coatings Company, a sister division, is a leader in marine and industrial coatings.

More Than Two Centuries of Quality

The company now known as Devoe & Raynolds began in 1754 when William Post opened a store on Water Street in New York City to sell his own ground pigments. The company's name came from the two men who managed it through the mid-1800s— C.T. Raynolds and F.W. Devoe.

Devoe became a part of the growing Louisville paint industry when, in 1928, it purchased the Peaslee-Gaubert Paint & Varnish Company. In 1938, Devoe increased its Louisville ties with its consolidation with Jones-Dabney Company of Louisville. The company headquarters was finally moved to Louisville in 1955. Devoe has a large national and international presence, serving customers in nearly every state and many overseas markets.

Devoe & Raynolds has about 1,000 employees nationwide. More than 300 of them work at 11 loca-

tions in the Louisville metropolitan area. The company's manufacturing site at Louisville Air Park on Grade Lane boasts one of the most efficient production and filling operations in the industry and serves dealers and company-owned stores in 17 states, including Kentucky. Along with the Louisville facility, Devoe's plants in Houston and Tampa supply paint and other products to more than 90 company-owned stores and over 900 independent dealers nationwide.

Research and development takes place at Devoe's Technical Center in west Louisville. It was at this center that Devoe invented the epoxy resin, a development that revolutionized the paint industry. Today, Devoe continues to develop advanced technology products, including many waterborne coatings that are environmentally friendly.

The home office is located at 4000 Dupont Circle in Louisville's east end, and houses staff operations for marketing, manufacturing, finance, personnel, and data processing.

Using Technology to Paint a Brighter Future

How does America's most experienced paint maker top itself after nearly two and a half centuries? By continuing to be the first company to introduce important innovations. "Yes, we're over 240 years old and we're proud of that," says Ron Raley, vice president-marketing. "But the reason we're still around is the quality and innovation of our products, backed by premium service and knowledgeable people. In fact, I would say our

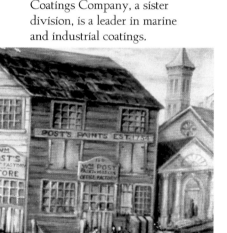

technology and R&D has been in overdrive in the past few years to meet today's technical demands in the painting industry."

Devoe introduced the first two-coat house paint in the early 1900s (others at that time required four coats). And in the 1940s, Devoe invented the epoxy resin, an important coatings and adhesive binder with widespread applications. More recently, Devoe has been a leader in waterborne coatings—an important and growing market because of environmental concerns about traditional solvent-based products. Devoe introduced the first splatterless latex paint in the early 1980s. And Devoe's MIRROLAC-WB™ is an advanced waterborne enamel that combines the adhesion and durability of oil-based paint with the safety of latex paint by using DEVCRYL™ resin technology developed at Devoe's Louisville Technical Center.

Another current innovation is THE COLOR KEY PROGRAM™ international color reference. This unique paint color system divides colors into two palettes: those based on blue undertones and those based on yellow undertones. THE COLOR KEY PROGRAM® helps architects, designers, and consumers select harmonious combinations of colors.

Adding Color to American History

During its own lengthy history, Devoe has contributed in significant ways to the nation's historic legacy. In the 19th century, the company was a leading supplier for the railroad industry and introduced the familiar Vermilion Red color used for cabooses. Devoe has been a leading supplier to historical areas such as New Orleans' French Quarter and historic homes in Charleston, South Carolina. According to Jane Ostertag, Devoe's advertising manager, the company has provided reproduc-

▶ DALE GEFFS

tions of Victorian home colors and even participated in a book on the subject. And Jackson Pollock, one of this century's best-known artists, used Devoe paint for his famous "drip" paintings.

Devoe paints also grace prestigious public buildings like the Houston Astrodome, the Hoosier Dome in Indianapolis, and the new Chicago Bulls' United Center. Devoe paint has also been used on Louisville landmarks, such as the *Belle of Louisville*, Galt House hotels, Freedom Hall arena, Cardinal Stadium, and Churchill Downs, the home of the Kentucky Derby.

From a tiny paint shop on New York's Water Street in 1754 to technological innovations for the 21st century, Devoe & Raynolds continues to paint a bright future for itself, Louisville, and the countless professionals and do-it-yourselfers who have come to rely on the company for superior paints and coatings.

THE COMPANY'S MANUFACTURING SITE AT LOUISVILLE AIR PARK ON GRADE LANE BOASTS ONE OF THE MOST EFFICIENT PRODUCTION AND FILLING OPERATIONS IN THE INDUSTRY AND SERVES DEALERS AND COMPANY-OWNED STORES IN 17 STATES, INCLUDING KENTUCKY.

J . J . B .   H I L L I A R D ,   W . L .   L Y O N S ,   I N C .

NE OF THE KEYS TO LONG-TERM SUCCESS FOR ANY BUSINESS IS establishing a clear sense of purpose. At J.J.B. Hilliard, W.L. Lyons, Inc., that sense of purpose is reflected in the company slogan: "Our Best Investment Is You." ◆ By remaining committed to the goal of making money for its clients, this investment firm has remained in business since

opening its doors in 1854. Today, Hilliard Lyons is the largest Kentucky-based securities firm in the Midwest and South. "Our staff of investment brokers handles more than a billion dollars in securities transactions each year," says Executive Vice President James R. Allen.

From Whiskey Receipts to the New York Stock Exchange

Hilliard Lyons traces its history to the decade before the Civil War when the booming trade along the Ohio River made Louisville the perfect location for the firm of Quigley and Lyons to establish a successful trade in gold shares and whiskey receipts.

Unfortunately, the Civil War split the partnership, just as it split many families. Henry L. Lyons, who sided with the South, continued the business under the name of Henry L. Lyons & Co. The company prospered, and in 1878 bought a seat on the New York Stock Exchange. The founder's son, W.L. Lyons, took over the firm after his father's death and renamed the firm W.L. Lyons & Company.

Meanwhile, in 1872 John James Byron Hilliard—whose plantation holdings in the Deep South had been wiped out in the war—joined two other businessmen to form A.D. Hunt & Company. The private banking firm accepted deposits and dealt in real estate mortgages, railroad bonds, the gold trade, and investment loans. In 1893 the name of the firm was changed to J.J.B. Hilliard & Son. The company

bought its own seat on the New York Stock Exchange in 1922. By the middle of the 20th century, it had become the dominant investment firm in the region.

During that time, W.L. Lyons & Company moved its main office to New York and, through an office in New Orleans, had become one of the country's largest cotton brokers. Commodities trading, along with securities brokerage, in both cotton and grain (on behalf of Louisville-area distillers and brewers) became one of the chief parts of the firm's business until 1952. At that time, the company decided to concentrate on the securities brokerage business. The company also moved its headquarters back to Louisville.

In 1965 the firm merged with J.J.B. Hilliard & Son and, in 1972,

THE OLDEST NEW YORK STOCK EXCHANGE MEMBER IN THE SOUTH, HILLIARD LYONS TRACES ITS HISTORY OF INVESTMENT IN THE SOUTHERN UNITED STATES TO BEFORE THE CIVIL WAR (RIGHT).

HILLIARD LYONS MAINTAINS STATE-OF-THE-ART FACILITIES AND EQUIPMENT (BELOW).

▼ GEOFFREY CARR

Hilliard Lyons shed its partnership status to become a corporation.

Personal Service for Individuals and Small Businesses

Although headquartered in Louisville, Hilliard Lyons has offices from Michigan to Mississippi, and from Missouri to North Carolina—an area considered the best location in the country for securities firms specializing in retail business. "We are a regional retail firm," Allen explains. "Our main thrust is careful attention to investments for individuals and small businesses. Our specialty has always been the individual client."

Throughout the firm, there is a quiet confidence that this niche will continue to fuel success in the future. In fact, when statistics of large New York-based firms and regional firms are compared, strong regional firms like Hilliard Lyons tend to outperform national ones in terms of return on investment for both shareholders and customers.

While retaining its regional, retail focus, Hilliard Lyons has always adopted the most sophisticated tools available and positioned itself to provide every investment service its customers need. The firm is not only the oldest New York Stock Exchange member in the South, it is also a member of most other major exchanges.

Preserving Community and Historic Ties

Perhaps because of its own long history, Hilliard Lyons has long demonstrated a keen appreciation of the history of the local communities in which it operates. For example, its current headquarters is in the historic Stewart's Dry Goods Building (renamed Hilliard Lyons Center) at the corner of Fourth Avenue and Muhammad Ali Boulevard, in Louisville's central business district. Many of the firm's branch offices are also located in buildings that have been placed on the National Register of Historic Places.

Hilliard Lyons also maintains a strong sense of corporate citizenship. Company officers stress the value of community activities with each new investment broker. And the firm as a whole has supported the Louisville community through charitable donations and securement of financing for public works projects. Among these projects are the Kentucky Center for the Arts, the Jefferson County Public Schools, the Standiford Field Airport expansion, and the University of Louisville.

Looking ahead, Hilliard Lyons intends to remain successful, though not necessarily by remaining the same. In fact, more than a century of experience has taught the firm that analyzing and managing change is one of the biggest services it can provide.

"Obliviousness to change is a costly state of mind," says Allen. "We try to help our clients stay on the plus side of change. The firm has survived every turn and cycle you can think of and remained profitable through it all."

THE SUCCESSFUL FINANCIAL FIRMS SHAPED BY J.J.B. HILLIARD (TOP PHOTO) AND W.L. LYONS (BOTTOM PHOTO) MERGED TO FORM HILLIARD LYONS IN 1965.

Brown & Williamson Tobacco Corporation

A SPECIAL RELATIONSHIP BETWEEN A COMPANY AND ITS community began on Saturday, January 26, 1929, when 54 people arrived in Louisville by train to report to work the following Monday at a small cigarette manufacturing plant on Hill Street. ◆ More than 65 years later, the Brown & Williamson Tobacco Corporation is one of Louisville's largest

and most international companies, with close to $3 billion in annual sales. Brown & Williamson occupies a prominent position along the city skyline, with corporate headquarters housed in a 26-story office tower in the heart of the downtown area.

Brown & Williamson—which celebrated the 100th anniversary of its founding in 1993—is the third-largest cigarette manufacturer in the United States and a leading exporter of international brands. The company employs about 5,800 people from its branch operations in eight cities, sales offices across the United States, and overseas offices in key global markets.

Commitment to Community

The 450 people who work at the company's headquarters are active in many different aspects of the community. Through the Louisville Employees Activities Program (LEAP), they have forged strong ties with such organizations as the Salvation Army, the Volunteers of America, the Muscular Dystrophy Association, and others.

American Red Cross officials know they can count on Brown & Williamson employees during crisis situations. During the great flood of 1937, B&W provided emergency shelter and food for hundreds of displaced families at its old facilities at 16th and Hill Street. Today, the Red Cross frequently conducts blood drives at the Brown & Williamson Tower.

In addition, employees often assume leadership positions, ranging from involvement in youth sports programs and church groups to board memberships for civic agen-

cies, volunteer organizations, and universities.

Brown & Williamson is equally committed to improving the Louisville-area quality of life. The company has a long tradition of assisting the economically, socially, and educationally disadvantaged through corporate contributions aimed at meeting the community's basic needs.

B&W strongly supports the Metro United Way and the Greater Louisville Fund for the Arts through employee-driven fundraisers and corporate contributions. Brown & Williamson is also a leading contributor to the United Negro College Fund. The Matching Gift program doubles employee contributions to accredited colleges and universities.

THE 26-STORY BROWN & WILLIAMSON TOWER IN DOWNTOWN LOUISVILLE SERVES AS THE CORPORATE HEADQUARTERS FOR THE COMPANY, WHICH CELEBRATED ITS 100TH ANNIVERSARY IN 1993.

NICHOLAS G. BROOKES IS THE CHAIRMAN AND CHIEF EXECUTIVE OFFICER OF THE BROWN & WILLIAMSON TOBACCO CORPORATION.

Bringing Innovation to the Market
B & W was founded in Winston-Salem, North Carolina, during the financial panic of 1893 by brothers-in-law George Brown and Robert Williamson. Hailing from families with deep roots in the tobacco industry, the young entrepreneurs were confident of success, despite the daunting economic conditions they faced.

In 1929 the company, which had been acquired by British-American Tobacco (B.A.T.), moved the bulk of its operations to Louisville to take advantage of its location as a distribution center and its close proximity to major burley markets.

B & W's rise to prominence has been built on creative and innovative marketing. KOOL, one of the industry's 10 top-selling cigarette brands, became the first menthol product to be marketed nationally in 1933. Viceroy featured the first cellulose acetate filter when introduced in 1952; the filter is now the industry standard. Capri was the first super-slim cigarette, ushering in an entirely new market segment in 1987.

The company also markets GPC, one of the industry's top generic

brands. Since B&W acquired the marketing rights to GPC in 1985, the brand has risen rapidly, capturing the number two position in 1995.

Other leading domestic cigarette brands include Carlton, Misty, Lucky Strike, Pall Mall, and Viceroy. Brown & Williamson also markets the Kent, Lucky Strike, KOOL, Capri, and Pall Mall brands internationally.

A second key to B & W's growth has been a strong emphasis on smoking quality. Achieving product superiority and unparalleled customer satisfaction is a top priority for B & W, which has taken many steps to bring the company closer to the consumer.

The centerpiece of these efforts is the Consumer Information Center. Brown & Williamson was the first firm in the industry to create a toll-free hotline to respond to consumer feedback. The center has become a catalyst for continuous product improvements. Suggestions and feedback from consumers are linked directly to customer-focused action and business results.

Throughout the company, investment in management information systems and other state-

of-the-art technology support Brown & Williamson's quality objective, enabling the company to respond rapidly to changes in consumer preferences and high levels of competition in the marketplace.

Promising Future
The 1994 acquisition of American Tobacco Company by B & W's parent company, B.A.T. Industries, makes B & W stronger than ever. The merger of the two companies increased B & W's market share by more than half, exceeding 17 percent of the domestic market.

The outlook for B & W, and the tobacco industry in general, is promising both at home and abroad. Growth opportunities abound for companies that apply creative and innovative approaches in meeting consumer preferences—a tradition that sets B & W apart from its competition and one that provides it with a basis for continued breakthroughs in the future.

THE CONSUMER INFORMATION CENTER SERVES AS A CATALYST FOR ACHIEVING SUPERIOR CONSUMER SATISFACTION. BROWN & WILLIAMSON WAS THE FIRST U.S. TOBACCO COMPANY TO PLACE A TOLL-FREE TELEPHONE NUMBER FOR CONSUMERS ON ALL ITS CIGARETTE PACKS AND CARTONS (ABOVE).

A KEY ELEMENT IN BROWN & WILLIAMSON'S PERFORMANCE MANAGEMENT PROGRAM IS PROVIDING CONTINUOUS TRAINING AND DEVELOPMENT OPPORTUNITIES FOR EMPLOYEES (BELOW LEFT).

KOOL, ONE OF THE INDUSTRY'S TOP-SELLING CIGARETTE BRANDS, BECAME THE FIRST MENTHOL PRODUCT TO BE MARKETED NATIONALLY IN 1933. OTHER BROWN & WILLIAMSON BRANDS INCLUDE KENT, LUCKY STRIKE, VICEROY, CAPRI, AND PALL MALL, TO NAME ONLY A FEW (BELOW).

▼ KEN KRAKOW

1930

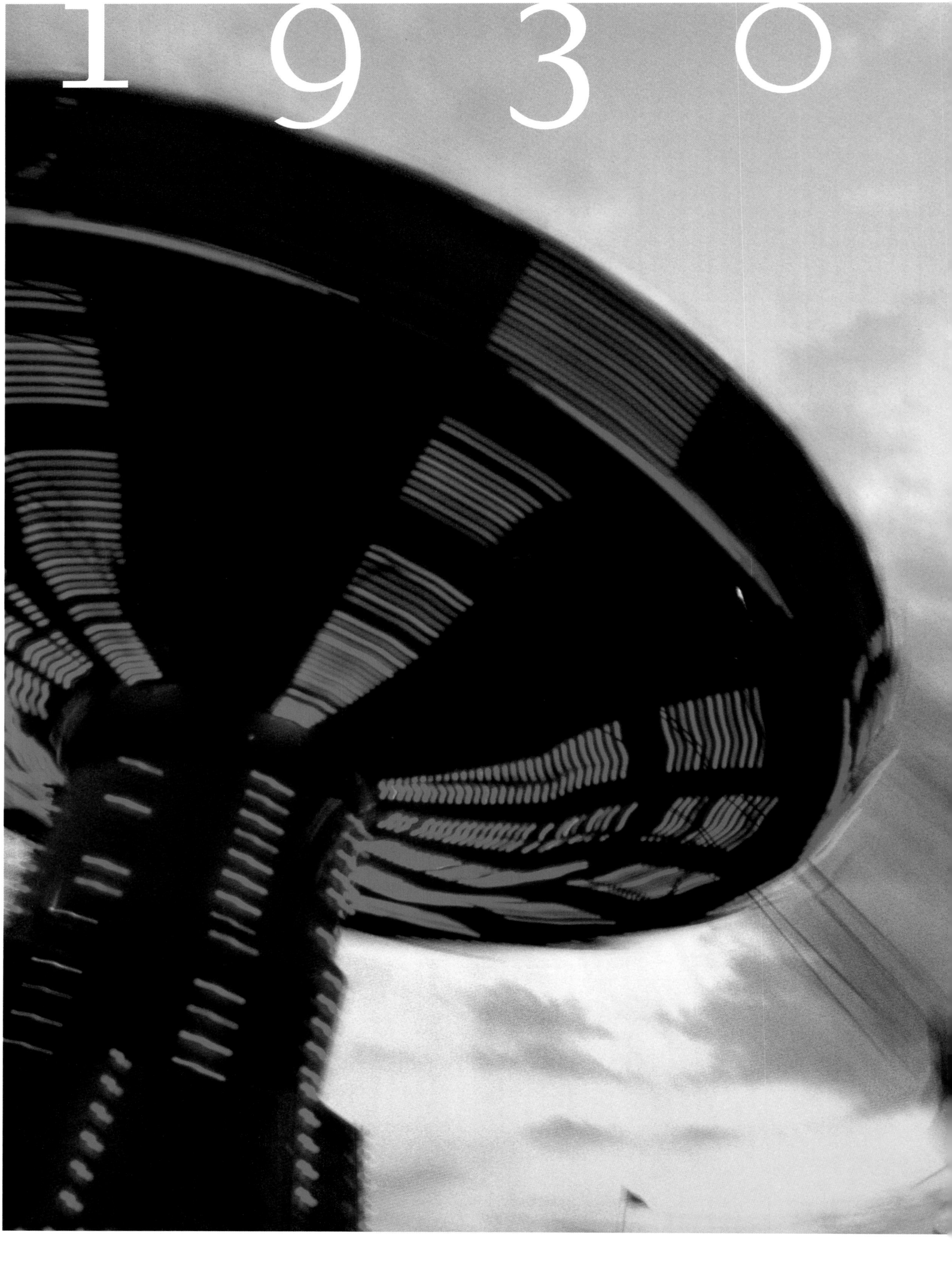

▲ © DAN DRY / DAN DRY & ASSOCIATES

1996

Dixie Warehouse & Cartage Co. 1938

E.I. Du Pont de Nemours & Co. 1941

Philip Morris Companies, Inc. 1944

Carrier Vibrating Equipment, Inc. 1948

WAVE 3 TV 1948

GE Appliances 1950

Louisville Area Chamber of Commerce 1950

American Synthetic Rubber Corporation 1954

Sandvik Sorting Systems 1956

Rohm and Haas Kentucky 1960

Humana, Inc. 1961

Sullivan Colleges System 1962

Airguard Industries, Inc. 1964

Providian Corporation 1969

Thornton Oil Corporation 1971

Wellness Institute, Inc. 1971

Borden Inc. 1973

Hurstbourne Hotel and Conference Center 1975

Power Graphics, Inc. 1976

United Catalysts, Inc. 1977

Hyatt Regency Louisville 1978

Greater Louisville Economic Development Partnership 1987

Prudential Service Bureau, Inc. 1988

ADVENT Environmental, Inc. 1992

Columbia/HCA Healthcare Corporation 1993

Acordia Personal 1994

Fifth Third Bank 1994

E. I. Du Pont de Nemours & Co.

*A*sk Community Relations Director Tim Martin about the Louisville operations of E.I. Du Pont de Nemours & Co., and you'll hear about more than just high-tech manufacturing or sales revenue. "One of our main goals, of course, is to be the low-cost producer in our industry," he maintains. "But I would say we have two other primary goals: to make this plant a safe place to work, and to be known as good corporate neighbors."

The Louisville plant and its 600 employees are succeeding in all three of these areas. Stretching toward the Ohio River in the city's "Rubbertown" area, Du Pont's Louisville Works is the largest and longest-operating producer of Neoprene—synthetic rubber. Invented by Du Pont in 1931, Neoprene's original cost was about 20 times as high as natural rubber. However, because the synthetic alternative did not deteriorate like rubber, it caught the eye of rubber product manufacturers who felt it was worth the price.

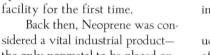

PRODUCTS MANUFACTURED FROM NEOPRENE INCLUDE GLOVES, HOSES, BELTS, GASKETS, AND SOLES FOR FOOTWEAR, TO NAME A FEW (RIGHT).

Valuable Resource in Wartime and Peacetime

The Louisville plant was originally built by Du Pont in 1941. However, before the company could begin production, the site was acquired by the U. S. government for the wartime production of Neoprene. The government established a contract with Du Pont to take over the operations. Eight years later, on January 1, 1949, the government returned the plant to Du Pont, and it was operated as a Du Pont-owned facility for the first time.

THE PLANT'S SAFETY ACTIVITY COMMITTEE DEVELOPS PROGRAMS TO IMPROVE EMPLOYEE AWARENESS AND OVERALL SAFETY PERFORMANCE FOR THE SITE (BELOW).

Back then, Neoprene was considered a vital industrial product—the only nonmetal to be placed on the U.S. government's priority materials list in World War II. Neoprene is now used in dozens of diverse applications. In industry, it is used for products like gas station hoses, power cables, automobile gaskets and fan belts, and nonflammable waterborne adhesives. For consumers, Neoprene can be found in sponges, mattresses, running shoes, running tracks, and garden hoses, among many other uses.

Today, the Louisville plant also houses a fluoroproducts division producing HCFC-22 and HFC-152a. Both products are used as refrigerants in applications such as air-conditioning systems and supermarket freezers. HCFC-22 is also the raw material for manufacturing Teflon®. Because HFC-152a is not a Volatile Organic Compound (VOC) and does not deplete ozone in the atmosphere, it is being used extensively as an aerosol propellant. The division also produces an intermediate used to make Tedlar®, a tough inert film used frequently in airplane interiors.

Together, these valuable products have made Du Pont a vital part of the Louisville economy. In 1994 the plant put nearly $50 million in wages into the pockets of local workers, and purchased more than $210 million in goods and services.

Good Citizenship Has Been a Family Affair

The Du Pont family left its mark on the city's history by establishing a public transit system, helping to create Central Park, and financing the construction of the Du Pont Manual High School.

It's only natural that Du Pont would strive to be a responsible corporate citizen of Louisville. One of the most visible ways the company lives up to its goal of responsible citizenship is by taking great care in the use and disposal of materials used in production—what Du Pont CEO Jack Krol has called "corporate environmental stewardship."

A good example is the way the Louisville Works handles hydrochloric acid. This chemical, a

by-product of HCFC-22 production, was once a difficult disposal problem. But since 1992, Du Pont has been able to find a market for all of the hydrochloric acid it produces.

Another important way Du Pont reaches out to the community is through its recently established community citizen advisory panel. According to Karl Turner, of the plant's Human Relations Office, the advisory council includes citizens from various interest groups in the community and discusses plant operation issues that might have a direct or indirect effect on Louisville-area residents. "It's our way of establishing a direct link between the community and the management here at the plant," Turner explains.

The Louisville Works is also an active financial contributor to many community-based programs, from the Metro United Way to the University of Louisville to the arts. The company has been particularly active in promoting youth and minority development efforts, such as the Black Achievers program.

Another Important Product: Safety

Although most industrial firms today are more aware of safety and environmental concerns than in the past, Du Pont can boast of nearly two centuries of safety-first attitudes. Martin notes that the first Du Pont factory was built on property adjacent to the residence of the company's founder. That, he explains, made E.I. Du Pont very conscious of safety concerns. "He would say that if we can't do it safely, we won't do it," says Martin.

So, along with its efforts to protect the environment, Du Pont spends a great deal of time and money protecting its workers. The Louisville plant has a Safety Activity Committee, with volunteer employee representatives from all areas of the operation. There is also a Central Safety Committee that establishes and monitors formal safety procedures. This proactive approach to safety has resulted in an accident rate that is significantly

below the industry average.

It's all part of Du Pont's long-term relationship with Louisville. "We've been here for five decades, and we'd like to be here for many more," says Martin. "To do that, we intend to behave in such a way that the community will not only allow, but want us to operate here."

LOCATED IN WESTERN JEFFERSON COUNTY, AND BORDERED BY THE OHIO RIVER, THE LOUISVILLE WORKS OPERATING FACILITIES OCCUPY MORE THAN 140 ACRES AND HAVE MANY MILES OF PROCESS PIPING.

AN OPERATOR INSPECTS A SHEET OF NEOPRENE FILM AS IT LEAVES A DRYER UNIT.

ROHM AND HAAS COMPANY

RENOWNED FOR A COMMITMENT TO INNOVATION AND QUALITY, Rohm and Haas Company manufactures chemicals used to create, mold, and strengthen hundreds of products worldwide. From its beginning in 1960 working out of an abandoned, war-era synthetic rubber plant rebuilt from the ground up, Rohm and Haas today employs 680 people. The company depends

upon the most sophisticated technology to produce four major product lines: plastics additives, acrylic coating resins, Plexiglas® molding resins, and emulsion products.

The Louisville facility is a part of Rohm and Haas Company, an international chemical manufacturer with 50 plants and 12,000 employees in all parts of the globe. Founded originally in Germany, Rohm and Haas has grown into a $3.5 billion corporation headquartered in Philadelphia.

Serving a Global Market
Rohm and Haas encompasses nine strategic business units that produce a wide variety of specialty chemicals with thousands of applications. The company is a leading supplier in the business-to-business segment, particularly in the paint, plastics, and consumer package goods industries. Rohm and Haas' ability to bring break-

through products to market enables it to successfully compete with larger firms, such as Dow, Du Pont, Monsanto, and Union Carbide. Plexiglas, first used in cockpit canopies in World War II, is a Rohm and Haas invention.

Products from the Louisville plant are found in all aspects of daily life. Plastics additives, for example, are used in home siding, plastic containers, and medical supplies. Acrylic resins go into solvent-based paints for cars, boats, and signage. Plexiglas molding resins make up taillight lenses, reflectors, and laser videodiscs. Emulsion products—of which Rohm and Haas is the world's number one producer—become part of acrylic paints, adhesives, floor polishes, and paper goods.

The company's innovative culture is due, in part, to its focused-factory manufacturing philosophy. Employees belong to self-managed work teams that are

responsible for developing schedules, assigning tasks, rotating functions, and overseeing the production process in accordance with corporate goals. The Louisville plant regularly plays host to observers from other organizations who consider Rohm and Haas a role model in the area of employee self-management.

Rohm and Haas has also invested considerable expertise in safeguarding its environment. In recent years, the plant has reduced solid, liquid, and airborne emissions, as well as adopted recyclable packaging for many of its products.

Active Members of the Community
Rohm and Haas is proud to be active in the community. "We're fortunate to be in a position to help," says Dan Hicks, manager of communications and public affairs. "Our goal is to be a good neighbor."

One example is the company's fully licensed and equipped on-site fire department. In addition to protecting the welfare of employees, the Rohm and Haas fire department supports local professional units, one of the few industry-owned departments in the nation to do so.

Rohm and Haas also emphasizes the importance of education through its annual scholarship awards to the best chemistry student in each nearby high school. Its Citizens Advisory Council provides a forum for the company to communicate with neighbors about their questions and concerns.

"The Rohm and Haas formula for business success—innovation, quality, teamwork—applies equally well to community relations," Hicks concludes.

ESSENTIAL ADDITIVES IN PLASTIC CONTAINERS FOR THE CONSUMER PACKAGE GOODS INDUSTRIES ARE ONE OF THE MANY PRODUCTS MANUFACTURED AT THE LOUISVILLE PLANT. ROHM AND HAAS HAS SUCCESSFULLY BROUGHT MANY BREAKTHROUGH PRODUCTS TO MARKET (BELOW TOP).

THE LOUISVILLE FACILITY IS ONE OF ROHM AND HAAS COMPANY'S 50 WORLDWIDE PLANTS. AN ABANDONED, WAR-ERA SYNTHETIC RUBBER PLANT WAS REBUILT FROM THE GROUND UP TO CREATE THIS MODERN FACILITY (BELOW BOTTOM).

◄ C.M. FREITAG

PHILIP MORRIS COMPANIES INC.

IN 1778 GEORGE ROGERS CLARK AND 150 SOLDIERS BUILT A FORT AT the hard-to-navigate rapids of the Falls of the Ohio. Over the next two centuries, that military post developed into Louisville, a bustling city of more than 250,000 people. ◆ Similarly, Philip Morris Companies Inc., the largest consumer packaged goods company in the world, has undergone substantial growth in the last two decades. Composed of the finest

tobacco, food, and beverage products, Philip Morris' portfolio has expanded with the addition of several subsidiaries during recent years.

Philip Morris USA—the tobacco division—manufactures and markets the highest quality cigarettes, including Marlboro, the world's best-selling cigarette; Merit; Benson & Hedges; Virginia Slims; Parliament; and Cambridge, among other brands.

The addition of Kraft in 1988 made Philip Morris the largest food company in the United States. The Kraft Foods Group produces household favorites such as Maxwell House, Jell-O, Kool-Aid, Post cereals, Breyers, Velveeta, and Miracle Whip, while the Oscar Mayer Foods division has become synonymous with the finest quality meat and poultry products.

The products of the Miller Brewing Company, the world's second-largest brewer, include both traditional brews, including Miller High Life, Miller Lite, and Miller Genuine Draft, and such recent additions as Red Dog, Icehouse, and Molson Ice.

Philip Morris USA and Louisville: A Winning Combination

Many people equate Philip Morris with Marlboro Country, yet Marlboro Country means different things to different people: thundering hooves of wild stallions, a cowboy settling down near a campfire. However you define it, Marlboro Country starts in Louisville, in the heart of tobacco country, where

Marlboro is produced.

Philip Morris USA has operated a manufacturing facility in this river city since 1944, creating an economic ripple effect throughout Kentucky. The largest manufacturing employer in Louisville and the eighth-largest in Kentucky, Philip Morris USA employs more than 2,400 people at its Maple Street facility. The company is also the largest purchaser of Kentucky burley tobacco, the state's leading cash crop. Flowing money into the economy, Philip Morris cigarettes sold in the Commonwealth generate more than $33 million annually from sales and excise taxes.

Philip Morris and its Louisville employees have provided a wide variety of community organizations with financial contributions and volunteer service. An example of the company's commitment to meeting the needs of its fellow Louisvillians is its annual Metro United Way campaign, which traditionally is among the community's most successful in generating combined employee and corporate contributions. Philip Morris employees also volunteer at local nonprofit organizations such as the Home of the Innocents, YMCA, Junior Achievement, and Big Brothers/Big Sisters.

For more than 35 years, the company has sponsored the Philip Morris Festival of Stars, the largest free-to-the-public, corporate-sponsored country music show in the nation and a major Kentucky Derby Festival event. The musical talent of entertainers such as Elvis Presley, Dolly Parton, Barbara Mandrell, Reba McEntire, John Michael Montgomery, and George Jones has been featured.

Just as construction of the McAlpine lock and dam cut a new course for the Ohio River to aid the river traffic that traverses its waters, Philip Morris Companies Inc. continues to recognize the rich cultural diversity of the community and is proud to call Louisville its home.

THE MANUFACTURING FACILITIES OF PHILIP MORRIS, LOCATED AT 18TH AND BROADWAY, PRODUCE A NUMBER OF QUALITY CIGARETTE BRANDS, INCLUDING MARLBORO, THE WORLD'S BEST-SELLING CIGARETTE (ABOVE).

◄ PATRICK L. PFISTER

PHILIP MORRIS USES STATE-OF-THE-ART TECHNOLOGY TO MANUFACTURE THE FINEST BLENDS OF TOBACCO PRODUCTS. HERE, THE MACHINES FILL CARTONS OF MARLBORO CIGARETTES TO BE SHIPPED AROUND THE WORLD (LEFT).

CARRIER VIBRATING EQUIPMENT, INC.

PROVIDING VIBRATING EQUIPMENT TO INDUSTRIAL CUSTOM-ers can be a challenging business, but Louisville-based Carrier Vibrating Equipment, Inc. has proved itself to be an industry leader that has passed the test of time for more than four decades. Internationally known for its pioneering work in the field of vibratory technology, Carrier Vibrating specializes in the manufacture of vibrating conveyors with features incorporated to screen, separate, dry, cool, blend, and perform various other processing functions while conveying.

A Pioneer Committed to Research and Development

In natural frequency vibration, a technology pioneered by Carrier, a free-vibrating spring and weight system is kept in motion with a relatively small force. In addition to moving, elevating, and feeding materials, vibrating conveyors can incorporate features to sort, classify, orient, and distribute within a wide range of industrial applications. By combining processing functions while moving products, heat transfer and chemical reactions are accelerated, and energy, time, and space are saved.

Carrier's sales and application engineers consult with prospective customers to develop, sell, and install equipment. The company's Vibranetics Division offers a full line of bin dischargers, pile dischargers, and screw feeders.

Because no two processing applications are exactly alike, no single solution works perfectly for all customers. Specialists tackle unique processing problems in Carrier's research and development lab, a complete test and demonstration facility where design concepts advance from the idea phase into viable, highly specialized processing operations. The lab offers a technology base in which customers, working jointly with Carrier engineers, can confidently test the feasibility of new products and processes, simulating actual operating conditions.

Carrier is dedicated to continuing the creation of better products at less cost by establishing more efficient techniques of manufacture, providing ongoing training to employees, finding competitive sources of quality materials, and exploring new markets.

In 1950 the company's founders, then operating under the name Whitley-Carrier Corporation, recognized an opportunity for patenting their inventions to harness vibration as a source of energy that would provide a highly functional form of movement. The new company set out to find market applications and manufacturing means for this new technology.

The next 30 years brought both rapid and incremental changes in vibration technology, with new products developed for the processing of chemicals, synthetics, glass, explosives, wood, coal, metals, scrap, and food. The company relocated to its present-day Fern Valley Road location in 1960, and greatly expanded its manufacturing facilities in 1974. From 1960 to 1980, sales grew 455 percent, and Carrier's technology bank increased substantially, with growth continuing to its present size of $35 million in annual sales worldwide.

In 1983 eight Carrier managers staked their own assets on continued profitability and orchestrated a leveraged buyout. In February

CARRIER'S MANAGEMENT TEAM INCLUDES MICHAEL DURNIL, MANAGER OF RESEARCH AND DEVELOPMENT ENGINEERING; KEN N. PATEL, PRESIDENT AND CEO; BRIAN TRUDEL, VICE PRESIDENT/SALES AND MARKETING; AND CHRIS SIMMS, VICE PRESIDENT/FINANCE AND OPERATIONS (RIGHT).

INNOVATIVE MANUFACTURING AND A COMPANYWIDE COMMITMENT TO QUALITY HAVE FUELED CARRIER'S GROWTH FOR MORE THAN 40 YEARS.

1990 two of the original eight owner/managers retired, and additional key employees were given the opportunity to buy stock in the company, which is currently headed by 16 owner/managers.

At present, Carrier employs 130 people at the Fern Valley Road location; operates subsidiary companies in Canada and Europe; maintains nearly 50 representative offices across the United States, Mexico, and Korea; and holds licensee agreements with companies in India, Japan, and Sweden.

The Incentive to Grow

Carrier has long recognized that people are the key factor in making potential a reality. The company has established a high-involvement environment in which key managers are motivated through active involvement in incentive profit sharing programs and succession planning strategies. Carrier's continued success is the result of its commitment to employees, suppliers, and customers, as framed in its mission statement: "Within the frame-

work of honesty and fairness, we will work as a team to stress caring and an atmosphere of camaraderie in all areas where employees interact with customers and with each other. Our Carrier team will deliver the highest-quality products and services, consistently, reliably, and profitably for all our customers, to provide the greatest value in the shortest period of time, with the goal to be first in our industry, while distinguishing ourselves in the global marketplace."

Carrier also realizes that it must give back to the community some of what it enjoys as profit. The company encourages employees to take community roles by supporting charitable and civic events, including active involvement in the Louisville Area Chamber of Commerce, the Louisville/Jefferson County Office of Economic Development, the March of Dimes, and many other local organizations. Carrier has been a sponsor of the Kentucky Derby Festival, and is a current sponsor of the Foster Brooks Pro-Celebrity Tournament and the

Louisville Homeless Benefit Ball.

Ken N. Patel, Carrier's president and chief executive officer, serves on the Industrial Board of Advisors for the University of Louisville's Speed Scientific School. The 30-member advisory board encourages stronger relationships between the university and all levels of industry, and ensures that the school's programs reflect rapidly changing industrial needs.

Carrier's phenomenal growth has occurred because of its capacity to bring new technology to market, as well as its ability to bring new value to existing technology. The company, working closely with customers on R&D projects and joint-development agreements, plans to maintain that pattern of growth in the future.

STATE-OF-THE-ART PRODUCTION TECHNIQUES UNDERSCORE CARRIER'S COMMITMENT TO DO IT RIGHT THE FIRST TIME, AND DO IT ON TIME (ABOVE).

CARRIER'S PRESIDENT AND CHIEF EXECUTIVE OFFICER IS K.N. PATEL (FAR LEFT).

THE COMPANY'S PRODUCT LINE INCLUDES VIBRATING CONVEYORS, FEEDERS, AND SPIRAL ELEVATORS, ALONG WITH FLUID BED DRYERS AND COOLERS—ALL CUSTOM DESIGNED FOR COST-EFFECTIVE PROCESSING.

WAVE 3 TV

BEING FIRST HAS A LONG TRADITION AT WAVE 3 TV. It started on the day before Thanksgiving in 1948 when WAVE-TV signed on the air as Kentucky's first television station. "We've been serving Louisville and the surrounding area, what we call WAVE Country, ever since," says Guy Hempel, vice president and general manager for the station. "Our dedication to

broadcast excellence and community involvement goes back to WAVE 3's founder and first president, George W. Norton Jr."

Under Norton's leadership WAVE 3 began a long history of being first in programming, news coverage, and technical innovations. From its early days the station provided live coverage of political elections, artistic performances, and sporting events. WAVE-TV was the area's first television station to broadcast basketball, football, hockey, boxing, and baseball—including the 1949 World Series. Earlier that same year WAVE-TV also televised the area's first broadcast of the legendary Kentucky Derby.

Local News Coverage—A Tradition of Innovations

"Our commitment to locally produced news programming began with Mr. Norton and continues to this day," says Hempel. "WAVE 3 takes great pride in being a leader in local and national news coverage." The station has supported its news reporting with technical innovations for more than four decades. In the 1960s WAVE-TV was the first local

broadcaster to maintain news bureaus in Frankfurt, Kentucky's state capital, and Washington, D.C. During this time, the station was the first to install a weather

radar system accompanied by the area's first local television meteorologist. Today WAVE 3's Meteorologist John Belski continues this tradition of forecasting

WAVE-TV WAS ONE OF THE FIRST LOUISVILLE STATIONS TO AIR LIVE PROGRAMMING IN THE EARLY DAYS OF BROADCASTING.

WAVE-TV'S TRADITION OF TECHNICAL INNOVATIONS INCLUDES THIS STATE-OF-THE-ART NEWS SET.

WAVE Country's ever-changing weather patterns. Belski combines his technical knowledge with a flavor for fun that has garnered him numerous awards as the area's favorite forecaster.

WAVE-TV's parade of firsts has marched on across the decades. In 1975 WAVE-TV was the first local station to hire a full-time consumer advocacy reporter, the WAVE 3 troubleshooter. In the 1980s Louisville's first hour-long newscast originated at WAVE 3, and in 1987 the station pioneered the area's first live satellite newscast.

Beyond local news coverage WAVE 3 has produced extensive children's programming over the years, including such classics as *Junior's Club* in the 1940s and *Funny Flickers* in the 1950s, along with a variety of popular presentations like *TV Opera Theater, Stop the Music,* and *The Pee Wee King Show.* Today WAVE-TV continues this tradition of local programming with weekly productions of *High Q, Urban Insight,* and *Time Out for Teens,* plus the annual Kentucky Derby Festival Pegasus Parade.

More Than a Broadcaster

WAVE 3's founder believed in serving the Louisville community in capacities beyond broadcasting. This conviction has continued even after the station was purchased by Cosmos Broadcasting Corporation in 1981. Since 1986 WAVE 3 has supported the local Salvation Army in mak-

ing its Angel Tree Project the most successful in the nation. The program provides clothing and toys for underprivileged children at Christmas and Hanukkah. During this holiday season, Christmas trees decorated with angels are placed at area malls. Each angel contains the wish list of a needy child. Shoppers are encouraged to adopt an angel and purchase that child's clothing or toys. The program has grown through time and now provides more than 18,000 children in WAVE Country with presents and warm holiday wishes.

In the same spirit of the holidays, WAVE 3 conducts a greeting card contest with area grade schools. Local students are encouraged to draw their vision of the season for the station. WAVE 3 receives thousands of drawings by these children, which makes it a difficult task for our panel of judges. Each year four winners are selected to have their artwork printed on WAVE 3 holiday cards, which are sent to the station's clients and to businesses across the country. The winning students receive a $100 U.S. Savings Bond and a set of their own professionally printed holiday cards to send to friends and family. Employees of WAVE 3 maintain the festive celebration of the season by lining the station's halls and offices with the remaining drawings.

In 1994 WAVE 3 created the S.T.E.P. Awards—Service Through Excellent Performance—recognizing outstanding African-Americans in Kentucky and southern Indiana during Black History Month in February. The S.T.E.P. Awards are presented to eight individuals who have given their time, effort, and dedication to the betterment of the community. A special award ceremony is held to honor these people who make a difference in our community and video profiles of these recipients are televised on WAVE 3.

The WAVE of the Future

For more than four decades WAVE 3 has held onto George Norton Jr.'s vision of a public-spirited enterprise dedicated to meeting the needs of the Louisville area. The station continues to set the standards for responsible news reporting, quality entertainment programming, and technical innovations. Working together with community leaders, assisting those in need, and providing a voice for local news and information are the pillars that support WAVE 3's theme "the spirit of WAVE Country."

LOUISVILLE'S FAVORITE FORECASTER, JOHN BELSKI, HAS A FLAVOR FOR FUN.

GE APPLIANCES

URING THE LAST QUARTER OF THE 19TH CENTURY, Thomas Edison formed nearly a dozen companies designed to manufacture, market, and distribute his many inventions—most notably the incandescent electric lamp. In 1890 he united his ventures to form the Edison General Electric Company. Seeking to resolve patent entanglements

with a competitor, the Thomson-Houston Company, Edison agreed to a merger in 1892 and the two rivals joined to create General Electric Company (GE).

On the forefront then just as it is today, GE demonstrated an early dedication to innovation and research. The company established the country's first industrial research laboratory in Schenectady, New York, in 1900. The stream of new technologies and products that emerged from the lab fueled GE's growth well into the early 20th century.

By 1950 GE executives were making optimistic predictions for burgeoning growth in the major appliance industry. The U.S. population was growing by 2 million per year. There had been significant increases in the number of homes wired for electricity. Per capita earnings were also on the rise, and it was reasonable to assume there would be high replacement demand for major appliances as new technology appeared and design improvements were implemented.

To meet the rising market demand, GE began looking for a location to manufacture appliances. The company selected Louisville—a site offering access to river, air, and rail transportation; an adequate labor supply; a favorable geographic location to serve as the hub of national distribution efforts; and a supportive business climate, which was fostered by state and local governments.

A New Kind of Park for Louisville

After the establishment of GE's local operations in 1950, the sleepy agricultural suburb of Buechel became an immense construction site the following year. In an effort to blend in with the rural surroundings, GE appropriated $100,000 for a massive landscaping effort. More than 400 acres were planted with grass, along with thousands of trees and shrubs in more than 700 varieties. Appliance Park became a reality.

From the beginning, GE promoted a good-neighbor policy in Louisville. The company supported local hospitals, youth organizations, and educational programs through donations and in-kind services. When the American Red Cross bloodmobile paid its first visit to Appliance Park in 1953, it discovered a wealth of enthusiastic donors. The bloodmobile would be back, and it would never leave empty-handed.

Also in 1953 the workers at Appliance Park elected the IUE-CIO labor union to represent their interests in negotiations with company management. Louisville and Appliance Park made "cyber-history" that same year when UNIVAC—the world's first computer system—was installed for its first industrial application. The enormous machine performed calculations relating to the company payroll, which took more than eight hours to complete.

Appliance Park made products that met the needs of families throughout the Eisenhower years and beyond. Building One produced home laundry equipment, Building Two rolled out electric ranges, Building Three dished out the dishwashers, and Building Four and Building Five manufactured refrigerators.

GE's Quality Commitment

Plenty of things have changed at Appliance Park more than 40 years after its founding, but the company's commitment to providing the highest-quality and most innovative products to consumers worldwide has remained constant. More than 7,300 hourly workers and 2,200 salaried workers based in Louisville contribute to the company's effort to manufacture and sell more than 10 million appliances each year in some 150 worldwide markets. Appliances carrying the brand names GE, Profile™, Monogram™, RCA, and Hotpoint account for a high proportion of GE's $5.5 billion in yearly appliance sales.

Since the first appliance rolled off the assembly line in Louisville in 1953, the company has also expanded the vast spectrum of products available at a wide range of prices, and has built the largest manufacturer's service organization in the appliance industry.

GE Consumer Service maintains a nationwide fleet of service vans to provide timely, high-quality repair and maintenance on all its branded appliances. The GE An-

GE APPLIANCES' PROFILE™ CLEANSENSOR DISHWASHER IS A STATE-OF-THE-ART MACHINE WITH AN ELECTRONIC SENSOR THAT ACTUALLY MEASURES THE SOIL LEVEL OF A DISH LOAD AND AUTOMATICALLY ADJUSTS WATER USAGE AND CYCLE LENGTH TO SAVE TIME, ENERGY, AND MONEY.

models. Top-of-the-line models offer 16 cycle selections and five fabric care selections to accommodate almost any kind of wash load. The Auto Balance System and deluxe insulation packages keep the newest product line quiet and reduce vibrations.

High-Tech Dishwashing

GE Appliances' CleanSensor dishwasher is a state-of-the-art machine with an electronic sensor that actually measures the soil level of a dish load and automatically adjusts water usage and cycle length to save time, energy, and money.

The dishwasher also features the SmartWash System, which provides three levels of wash action; the CircuClean pump for improved wash performance; and the GE Profile QuietMotor, active venting system, and insulation package for excellent sound reduction and a quiet run.

"The CleanSensor dishwasher is a true innovation that will offer consumers tangible benefits," says Paul Bossidy, general manager of dishwashers. "A dishwasher that knows how long it will take to get dishes clean takes less time to do its job and saves significant amounts of energy and water. Those reductions in the use of energy and water save the consumer money and help contribute to a better environment."

The new line comes in three monochromatic, sleek colors—white-on-white, black-on-black, and almond-on-almond—to integrate with a variety of kitchen designs.

Kitchen Appliances for Today's Meals

The GE Profile series of appliances also offers consumers a line of Smart Refrigerators, Clean-Design Cooktops, and built-in single and double ovens.

Refrigerators come in all shapes and sizes, but only GE Appliances offers the world's largest, freestanding model: The

MORE THAN 7,300 HOURLY WORKERS AND 2,200 SALARIED WORKERS BASED IN LOUISVILLE CONTRIBUTE TO THE COMPANY'S EFFORT TO MANUFACTURE AND SELL MORE THAN 10 MILLION APPLIANCES EACH YEAR IN SOME 150 WORLD-WIDE MARKETS (ABOVE).

TOP-OF-THE-LINE GE PROFILE WASHERS OFFER THE UNIQUE AUTO BALANCE SYSTEM AND DELUXE INSULATION PACKAGES TO REDUCE VIBRATIONS FOR A QUIETER RUN (RIGHT).

INNOVATIVE USE OF SPACE AND SLEEK DESIGNS MAKE GE APPLIANCES ATTRACTIVE, EFFICIENT ADDITIONS TO ANY HOME (OPPOSITE).

swer Center®, based in Louisville, fields approximately 3 million calls each year from consumers with product information or repair questions. Its toll-free number, 800-626-2000, is answered 24 hours a day, 365 days a year.

Appliances for Every Need

From its facility at Appliance Park, GE Appliances manufactures a wide variety of laundry products, electric ranges, dishwashers, and top-mount no-frost refrigerators. Among the company's most recent additions to

its product line are its Profile washers and the Profile™ Clean-Sensor dishwasher—both made in Louisville.

The GE Profile washer features the industry's largest capacity—3.2 cubic feet—and a new suspension system that virtually eliminates noise from off-balance loads. Not only are the washers functional, but in keeping with today's trend of incorporating laundry space into the upstairs or living quarters of a house, the new models sport a stylistic, unique design.

GE listened to consumers to create a product that addresses the laundry needs of today. "No one particularly likes to do the laundry. These machines make it a much more manageable chore," says Brian Kelley, GE Appliances' general manager for laundry products. "Our goal in the design and execution of the new GE Profile washers was to make every aspect of washing clothes easier and more effective."

The proof is in the numbers. With 3.2 cubic feet of capacity, load sizes can be increased enough to avoid doing up to 75 extra loads per year—a savings of 80 hours in laundry time versus prior GE

GE Profile 30. It provides 30 cubic feet of food storage space, and the ingenious SmartDesign! concept puts the space where it is needed—on the inside, not the outside.

Profile series side-by-side refrigerators boast an innovative design including an ice and water dispenser in the door, QuietSound noise reduction packaging, and a Nice Cubes™ ice maker that provides rounded-shape ice to reduce ice clogging when drinking beverages.

CleanDesign cooktops provide a flat, smooth surface for easy cleaning. Beneath-the-surface burners are available in either halogen or ribbon heating units. Baking needs can be met through one of GE Appliances' versatile convection ovens. The ovens' flush appearance allows it to integrate with the surrounding cabinetry for a sleek, contemporary design that fits into any kitchen.

Welcome to the Future

What started as a folly became a foundation for phenomenal growth for both Louisville and GE. By remaining true to the principles of innovation established by Thomas Edison, great leaps of progress have been made in the five decades that span the history of Appliance Park. Even greater leaps are just beyond the horizon, and GE is counting on Louisville to play an important role in the progress to come.

As GE Appliances President and CEO Dick Stonesiter says, "If we have learned our lessons from the past, we must be the world's leader in quality and cost to win. We know we can meet that goal by working together toward our vision to be 'one team better and faster than anybody else in the world.'"

*T*WO BLOCKS SOUTH OF THE RIVER THAT CARVED LOUISVILLE'S PAST is an organization at work forging the region's future—the Louisville Area Chamber of Commerce. ◆ Much like the mighty Ohio of yesteryear, today's Chamber promotes commerce, influences community development, and serves as a natural resource for business. Its ongoing efforts to build a foundation for regional growth and competitiveness have

MUCH LIKE THE MIGHTY OHIO OF YESTERYEAR, TODAY'S CHAMBER PROMOTES COMMERCE, INFLUENCES COMMUNITY DEVELOPMENT, AND SERVES AS A NATURAL RESOURCE FOR BUSINESS.

helped the community turn the corner—and turned a few heads in the process.

In 1995, for instance, Greater Louisville was named one of 10 "All-America Cities," based in part on Chamber initiatives. In the same year, The Chamber earned an "Excellent Rating" from the U.S. Chamber of Commerce and an "Equality Award" from the Louisville Urban League to go with its 1994 honors as "Best Supporter of Entrepreneurism" (Regional Entrepreneur of the Year Awards) and Award for Excellence winner from the National Association for Membership Development.

The organization seems to earn accolades as often as the river bends. What's the secret?

"The Chamber has accepted one challenge after another and now is looked to for leadership on important economic and community issues," says Bob Gayle. The Chamber's president and CEO. "At the same time, we continue to provide targeted services to help businesses grow and use the input of business and community leaders to continually adapt and improve our product."

The organization, whose history includes mergers with other associations as well as the creation of offshoot entities in such areas as business attraction, has today evolved into an economic development leader. The Chamber manages the Regional Economic Development Strategy, the region's long-range blueprint for growth and competitiveness. It is considered a major "player" in the community decision-making process.

"This is not your grandfather's chamber of commerce," says Gayle. "Times change and so do the needs of business and the community. Like any business in a competitive environment, a chamber must constantly adapt and improve its products and services or run out of customers."

Chamber Plays a Leading Role in Commerce

Flatboats are out. Laptops are in. And Chamber efforts to facilitate commerce have evolved, too, over the past century. The Chamber is now a partner with other local economic development agencies through a unique memorandum of understanding. It works with the Kentucky World Trade Center to maximize international business opportunities. And, it is tapped into the Internet to provide global exposure for its members.

Of course, providing business contacts and networking opportunities is still a key Chamber service. Monthly Business Breaks take members to the newest and hottest locations in Greater Louisville. Area Council breakfast meetings link Chamber services and representation to the region's outlying areas. Trade shows, seminars, and one-on-one counseling provide valuable services for member firms.

"My company has found The Chamber to hold a wealth of resources, from excellent business contacts to training seminars to networking opportunities," says Agnes Sellers Stewart, president of Incentives, Inc.

Around the Bend: Community Development

Greater Louisville's economic development started at the riverbanks. Today, it has swelled over to include the entire community and region. And, factors critical to development—including gov-

tiative that incorporates FastTrac I and II, the nation's premier training program for entrepreneurs and new business owners.

"For years, The Chamber has been the premier source for training and development programs designed to make growing companies smarter," says Doug Cobb, president of Chrysalis Ventures. "The entrepreneur initiative fills a missing piece of the puzzle by encouraging the creation and development of new businesses.

Rolling Like a River

What happens when an organization—just a stone's throw from the river—starts making a few ripples?

As a result of The Chamber's "new and improved" product, the nonprofit business association has enjoyed a 60 percent membership increase since 1991 and now serves more than 3,000 member businesses. And—not coincidentally— the local economy continues to grow and add jobs at a rate that exceeds the national average.

The Chamber works for Greater Louisville. In the 1990s, one could say that the organization has even put itself on the map.

FROM ITS OFFICES ON MAIN STREET, THE CHAMBER—WORKS WITH OTHER ECONOMIC DEVELOPMENT ORGANIZATIONS AT COMMERCE CENTER (LEFT).

GREATER LOUISVILLE'S ECONOMIC DEVELOPMENT STARTED AT THE RIVERBANKS, BUT SWELLED OVER TO INCLUDE THE ENTIRE COMMUNITY AND REGION (ABOVE).

ernment advocacy, workforce development, and infrastructure planning—are now an integral part of The Chamber's mission.

The Chamber's government advocacy action during recent years helped defeat tax proposals, attain state funding for local capital projects, create tax reforms, and privatize Naval Ordnance Station Louisville. The Chamber-coordinated Governance study produced recommendations to deliver government services more efficiently. And, workforce development initiatives have set in motion a system that will deliver a skilled workforce to this community for years to come.

In addition, The Chamber helped coordinate the Land Use and Infrastructure Plan that will provide a blueprint for orderly growth and

development throughout the county. The organization is actively involved in the bridge study process and is seeking to meet clean air standards without severely penalizing businesses.

"Quality of life is just as important as the strength of the business community when a region is trying to compete with other regions all over the world," says Vic Staffieri, president of Louisville Gas & Electric Company.

A Natural Resource for Business

Whether the year is 1950 or 2050, The Chamber—just like the Ohio River—will continue providing resources for local businesses.

The newest addition is an entrepreneurial development ini-

A MERICAN SYNTHETIC RUBBER CORPORATION, ONE OF ONLY four manufacturers of polybutadiene rubber in the country, got its start in Louisville in 1943 as a government-owned factory producing synthetic rubber for the nation's needs during World War II. While its staple product today is the synthetic rubber used in tires, American Synthetic has

FROM ITS LOUISVILLE PLANT AMERICAN SYNTHETIC PRODUCES 1 MILLION POUNDS OF SYNTHETIC RUBBER A DAY.

expanded into new fields, including production of a liquid polymer used as a solid fuel binder in NASA's space shuttle program.

American Synthetic produces 1 million pounds of synthetic rubber a day in the form of polybutadiene rubber (PBR) and solution styrene butadiene rubber (SSBR). In its early days during World War II, the Louisville plant boasted a production capacity of 60 million pounds per year. But at the war's end, the U.S. government put the facility on standby status and it remained closed until the early 1950s. A company called Kentucky Synthetic Corporation was formed in 1953 and took over the

plant. Kentucky Synthetic became American Synthetic Rubber Corporation a year later.

Industry Leader

American Synthetic is clearly dedicated to its industry, a fact evident in the company's long-term participation in many professional organizations, such as the American Institute of Aeronautics and Astronautics, American Society for Quality Control, Chemical Manufacturers' Association, and Rubber Manufacturers' Association. It has also assumed a leadership role in the International Institute of Synthetic Rubber Producers.

In its industry, American Synthetic's greatest successes have resulted from the company's ability to implement the latest in technology. Modifications to its polybutadiene facility enabled the plant to produce a proprietary SSBR process for the tire industry. The changes American Synthetic engineered brought the company up to operating capacity in less than 24 months from the project's inception.

American Synthetic plans to continue supplementing its product line with the most current technology available. Its participation in the Edison Polymer Innovation Corporation (EPIC), associated with the University of Akron and Case

Western Reserve University, assures the company access to new ideas and the facilities to pursue its own innovations.

Placing Customer Satisfaction Foremost

Working relationships—whether with customers, employees, or suppliers—receive special emphasis at American Synthetic. The company's 390 employees display an air of ownership and concern about the plant and its business. The company, in turn, provides an atmosphere of cooperation and opportunities for employee involvement.

Recently initiated incentives encourage employees to improve safety performance. The success of the program led to the institution of a variety of personal and work-related incentive programs that allow employees to pursue their interests in stress management, weight loss, tobacco cessation, and physical fitness. American Synthetic continues to encourage education and training by offering benefits for tuition and a variety of opportunities for operators. In this manner, the company acknowledges its primary commitment to its employees and their continued well-being.

Environmental Steward

A large portion of American Synthetic's efforts and resources are currently being directed toward its energy and environmental requirements. As a Responsible Care® company, American Synthetic is committed to being a true steward of natural resources. The company invests its resources to further that commitment and voluntarily participates in the federal Environmental Protection Agency's 33/50 program to reduce emissions. American Synthetic has reduced emissions by almost 80 percent since 1990.

In addition, the company's steam plant has incorporated fea-

tures allowing it to utilize available resources to improve the plant's efficiency while supplying steam. By incorporating the newest technology available and the capability to thermally destroy organic emissions derived from the rubber-production process, American Synthetic has significantly improved the overall air quality in the region with this project.

In order to minimize the impact of its operations on the local environment, American Synthetic has taken innovative approaches to address these concerns. Biological treatment of effluent streams, programs for waste-to-energy conversion, and further integration of energy and emission streams continue to provide significant improvements in its operations and in the quality of life for its neighbors and for the community at large.

American Synthetic's commitment to the Louisville area includes cosponsoring a community advisory panel, as well as participation in many service activities, such as the United Way, Urban League, Junior Achievement, Louisville Science Center, and co-op programs with

University of Louisville in engineering and chemistry.

Whether producing liquid polymers for the space shuttle program or discovering more environmentally friendly production methods, American Synthetic Rubber Corporation will continue to be an asset to the Louisville community well into the next century.

WORKING RELATIONSHIPS—WHETHER WITH CUSTOMERS, EMPLOYEES, OR SUPPLIERS—RECEIVE SPECIAL EMPHASIS AT AMERICAN SYNTHETIC (TOP).

AS A RESPONSIBLE CARE® COMPANY, AMERICAN SYNTHETIC'S PLANTS ARE COMMITTED TO BEING TRUE STEWARDS OF NATURAL RESOURCES (BOTTOM).

Y OU MIGHT BE SHIPPING A BIRTHDAY GIFT FOR YOUR NIECE OR AN important set of business documents. Or perhaps you are returning an item ordered from a catalog. Once your parcel is picked up by the delivery company, it becomes just one of many hundreds of thousands, even millions, of parcels to be handled that day. How does your package arrive at the right place, on time? Sandvik Sorting Systems, Inc., headquartered in

Louisville, plays a major role in this rather amazing feat.

From Sweden to Louisville

Sandvik Sorting Systems is a subsidiary of the Sandvik Group, a Swedish entity with about 30,000 employees in some 60 countries around the world. The Sandvik Group began as a steel company in 1862. Today, it is a diversified materials technology company with an international focus.

When Sandvik sought a strong U.S. presence for its sorting business, Louisville was chosen from among several cities across the country. In 1991 Sandvik acquired Seamco, a Louisville-based manufacturer of material-handling equipment. Seamco, which began in Louisville in 1956, possessed the precise combination of experience and commitment to service that Sandvik sought. Louisville was a good location due to a highly quali-

fied workforce and its proximity to Sandvik's major customers.

Today, Louisville is home to about 200 of some 250 Sandvik Sorting Systems employees, among them some of the industry's most skilled engineers and technicians. Sandvik draws on the experience of its people, while encouraging con-

tinuous learning, to achieve its goals of constant innovation and market leadership in the automated sorting industry. Sandvik Sorting Systems headquarters is located at a newly designed office and manufacturing facility near the University of Louisville Belknap campus.

Delivering Solutions

So, what exactly happens to the parcel that you sent? After your parcel is picked up, chances are it is taken directly to an automated sorting facility, where it joins hundreds of thousands of other parcels destined for locations all over the world. The parcels must then be sorted by country, region, state, or city, and so on, before being loaded back onto another truck or plane. This entire process takes place during a very short period of time. Especially in the case of overnight deliveries, time is of the essence.

Sandvik has helped to transform the parcel-sorting process, which once was accomplished solely through manual labor, into a very efficient process. The automated systems that Sandvik installs in these and other sorting facilities increase the speed and accuracy of the sorting process, and decrease workplace injuries. Automated sorting systems have also enabled faster and earlier parcel delivery than ever before.

Sandvik Sorting Systems handles its sorting system projects from start to finish. It has the necessary expertise in engineering, manufacturing, and installation to get the job done. Based on its unique steel belt technology, Sandvik tailors its sorting systems to the needs of its

WHEN SWEDEN-BASED SANDVIK SOUGHT A STRONG U.S. PRESENCE FOR ITS SORTING BUSINESS, LOUISVILLE WAS CHOSEN FROM AMONG SEVERAL CITIES ACROSS THE COUNTRY (RIGHT).

BASED ON ITS CUSTOMER-FOCUSED SOLUTIONS APPROACH, SANDVIK MAINTAINS ITS INNOVATIVE EDGE (BOTTOM).

customers in the parcel delivery industry and beyond.

Sorting It All Out

The sorting facilities into which the Sandvik systems are installed vary by size and layout. One large system engineered and installed by Sandvik consists of more than 60 miles of conveyor belting, and sorts more than 2.8 million parcels per day. Imagine parcels lined up end-to-end from Louisville to Buffalo, New York, and you will get an idea of the kind of volume the system handles. The building containing this system is roughly equivalent in square footage to 42 football fields! To ensure continuous operation, some 80,000 points are electronically monitored by a computerized system.

Inside the sorting facility, parcels are processed by specialized scanners and automatic sorting devices that assess parcel dimensions, space parcels evenly, read coded labels affixed to the parcels, and guide them to the appropriate destination. The parcels may travel at speeds of more than 500 feet per minute. A tremendous amount of information is also generated by a sophisticated computer that drives the system and provides instant tracking of parcels.

Customer-Driven Innovations

Sandvik prides itself on the creative use of advanced technology, constantly developing and improving upon designs to bring better sorting solutions to its customers. One example of this kind of approach is a remarkable Sandvik product that was designed to take a mass of parcels and line them up in a single file for easy sorting.

This new product, called the Linear Singulator™, was so innovative that two engineers from Sandvik's Louisville facility received the Haglund Medal for its development. The Haglund Medal is the Sandvik Group's top award for innovation among its many companies worldwide.

Based on its customer-focused solutions approach, Sandvik maintains its innovative edge. In fact, Sandvik Sorting Systems has averaged two patents per year, helping its customers to become more efficient—and improve their business position—through the use of automated sorting technology.

Sandvik Sorting Systems is proud to be a part of the beautiful Louisville community, with its equestrian heritage and cultural opportunities, and pleased to benefit from the community's strong economic growth and bright future.

THE AUTOMATED SYSTEMS THAT SANDVIK INSTALLS IN SORTING FACILITIES INCREASE THE SPEED AND ACCURACY OF THE SORTING PROCESS AND DECREASE WORKPLACE INJURIES (TOP).

SANDVIK HAS HELPED TO TRANSFORM THE PARCEL-SORTING PROCESS, WHICH ONCE WAS ACCOMPLISHED SOLELY THROUGH MANUAL LABOR, INTO A VERY EFFICIENT PROCESS (BOTTOM).

HUMANA INC.

FROM AN INITIAL INVESTMENT OF $6,000 TO ITS CURRENT position as one of America's premier managed health care companies, Humana Inc. has been one of Louisville's greatest business success stories. In the three decades since it was founded, two themes have never changed: the company's belief in creative approaches to delivering excellent service and its equally

strong commitment to staying deeply rooted in the Louisville community.

Cofounder and Chairman David Jones, a Louisville native, is almost as well known for his civic activities as for his leadership role at Louisville's largest homegrown corporation. Humana's headquarters, designed by noted architect Michael Graves, has become a distinctive part of Louisville's downtown skyline. *Time* magazine called the

Humana Building the single most significant piece of American architecture built in the 1980s.

A Vision of Excellence through Measurable Quality

Throughout its history, Humana has been involved in numerous health care activities and has been successful in each of them due to its commitment to high-quality service. Humana's expertise has evolved to the point that it focuses entirely on health care plans and services. Humana manages care, not nursing homes or hospitals. But its success in these earlier efforts has helped it become one of the nation's largest, publicly traded managed care companies.

"With our experience in so many aspects of the health care industry—hospitals and nursing homes included—we've accumulated an enormous amount of know-how in the delivery of quality," says Wayne T. Smith, president and COO.

The Humana story began when Jones and cofounder Wendell Cherry, who died in 1991, created a company called Extendicare. Jones, Cherry, and four friends invested $1,000 each to start one of the first nursing homes to provide personal attention to patients. Extendicare eventually grew from a single nursing home in Louisville to become the largest company of its type in America, with more than 40 facilities.

In 1968 the company purchased its first hospital—Medical Center Hospital in Huntsville, Alabama. Jones and Cherry embarked on an effort to revamp the health care delivery system by using the principle of quality con-

trol that was revitalizing other industries. Renamed Humana in 1974, the company managed more than 80 hospitals at home and abroad during the 1980s.

Humana's vision of excellence led to the Centers of Excellence program, founded in 1982, which came to symbolize Humana's mastery in delivering quality. Hospitals designated as Centers of Excellence supplemented innovative care in one or more specialties with teaching and research efforts. All of Humana's hospitals were accredited, 71 percent with commendation. The national average for commendation is 5 percent. The Humana Heart Institute International in Louisville captured the world's attention with its critical research involving the artificial heart.

Corporate Citizen and Problem Solver

Humana employs thousands of people and serves hundreds of thousands of health plan members in the Louisville area. In addition, the company is vitally involved in the overall life of the community. "Anything that can be done anywhere can be done in Louisville," says Jones. This attitude has resulted in Humana's becoming one of Louisville's leading corporate citizens, proudest boosters, and most innovative problem-solvers.

In 1983 the company formed a remarkable partnership that virtually eliminated Louisville's indigent medical care problem. Humana negotiated an agreement with the University of Louisville and with local and state government to provide care for indigents at the university's teaching hospital. In

return for providing care and managing the facility, Humana received a limited amount of public money, which it shared with the University of Louisville School of Medicine. By putting the hospital back on sound financial footing, Humana demonstrated a unique commitment to the health of its hometown.

Since 1981 Humana has been the sole sponsor of the internationally recognized Humana Festival of New American Plays, produced annually by Actors Theatre of Louisville. Cherry played a pivotal role in the development of the Kentucky Center for the Arts, home to cultural events ranging from Broadway shows to experimental theater. And Jones' efforts led to the relocation of the Presbyterian Church USA's international headquarters to Louisville.

First to See the Future
In 1984 Humana offered its first group health care plans and services, thus beginning the company's transformation from a hospital firm into one of the nation's leaders in managed health care. Humana was one of the first companies to see the threat that inflation held for the affordability of group health care coverage.

Managed care offers covered services through physician and hospital networks that practice quality, cost-effective medicine. It emphasizes wellness through preventive care services such as physicals and well-baby care. Humana's early managed care plans encompassed a variety of design options, including preferred provider organizations (PPOs) and health maintenance organizations (HMOs), as well as modified indemnity plans. The company also introduced Medicare supplement and HMO policies for individual retirees.

Humana's managed care plans were immediately popular. By 1988 more than 750,000 people were enrolled in Humana Health Care Plans. In 1993 Humana spun off its hospital division as a separate company. Humana today is one of the nation's premier managed care companies with a plan membership of nearly 4 million people and anticipated revenues of some $6 billion in 1996.

Making Quality Care Affordable
In addition to PPOs, HMOs, and Medicare products, Humana's portfolio of managed care plans has grown to include exclusive provider organizations (EPOs); point-of-service (POS) plans; workers' compensation products; and ancillary benefits such as dental, vision, and hearing care coverage. The company also caters to the needs of government employees with federally qualified HMOs and military health care (CHAMPUS) plans.

In every case, quality is the overriding concern. This is especially apparent in Humana's dedication to service. The Service Excellence Department maintains a quality-measurement program with demanding guidelines. Humana invested $12 million in an optical character recognition (OCR) computer system that drastically improves the speed and accuracy of claims processing.

The company's expertise is such that it has become a third-party administrator offering claims processing, enrollment, and billing services as well as a 27,000-member provider network to self-insured groups around the country.

At the same time, Jones is working for better health care on a national scale. He serves as a member of the Business Roundtable on Health, Welfare and Retirement Income Task Force. He is a founder and past chairman of the Healthcare Leadership Council and a past member of the Jackson Hole Group.

The company has remained true to the original vision of Jones and Cherry. Humana means affordable access to quality care.

HUMANA CHAIRMAN AND CEO DAVID A. JONES (RIGHT) AND PRESIDENT AND COO WAYNE T. SMITH HAVE GUIDED HUMANA THROUGH A RECENT PERIOD OF DRAMATIC GROWTH AND IMPROVED CUSTOMER SATISFACTION (LEFT PHOTO).

RENOVATED AND RENAMED HUMANA WATERSIDE IN 1990, HUMANA'S HISTORIC RIVERFRONT COMPLEX HOUSES MORE THAN 2,000 LOCAL HUMANA EMPLOYEES (BELOW).

▼ PATRICK PFISTER

*M*EETING CUSTOMER NEEDS WITH HIGH-QUALITY PRODUCTS and services is the goal of virtually every organization. In Louisville, the institutions that comprise the Sullivan Colleges System have been meeting the area's career education needs for more than a century, training students for the jobs in demand right now. ◆ Sullivan College

was originally established as a one-year school of business in 1962. The founders, A.O. Sullivan and A.R. Sullivan, were career educators with a history in postsecondary business education in Louisville since 1926.

Since its founding, the college has undergone many significant changes. In 1972 it received the authority to offer two-year associate degrees. Sullivan merged in 1973 with Bryant & Stratton Business College, whose history dates back to 1864.

In 1979 Sullivan became the first private career college in the South to receive accreditation from the Commission on Colleges of the Southern Association of Colleges and Schools at the associate degree level. Sullivan added a baccalaureate degree program to its one- and two-year programs in 1990, which received accreditation effective January 1, 1992.

While broadening its degree programs, Sullivan also has expanded geographically. In 1982 the college began offering extension

THE VARIETY OF PROGRAMS AVAILABLE IN THE SULLIVAN COLLEGES SYSTEM REFLECTS A CONTINUOUS EFFORT TO ADAPT TO THE CHANGING ECONOMY AND TEACH SKILLS REQUIRED FOR CAREER SUCCESS (RIGHT).

LOUISVILLE TECH, A MEMBER OF THE SULLIVAN SYSTEM, OFFERS PROGRAMS OF STUDY INCLUDING MARINE MECHANICS TECHNOLOGY, COMPUTER-AIDED DESIGN AND DRAFTING (CADD), AND COMPUTER ENGINEERING TECHNOLOGY (BELOW).

programs in Fort Knox to serve both the military and civilian populations. A second branch campus was opened in Lexington in 1985.

A Growing System

The Sullivan Colleges System also includes Spencerian College and Louisville Technical Institute. The emphasis at all three institutions is the same: to provide practical course work designed to build a foundation for each student's future career.

Spencerian College, founded in 1892 by Enos Spencer, has long been recognized as a leading name in business education. In *Beginning of the Business School*, author Charles G. Reigner notes, "The name Spencerian has embedded itself in the consciousness of the American people . . . it is an honored name." Spencerian specializes in the medical and business fields, offering degrees in vocations such as business office manager, microcomputer accounting specialist, clinical assistant, practical nursing, and medical transcriber.

Louisville Technical Institute (known as Louisville Tech) was established in 1961 by George Dumbaugh, a professional engineer. Dumbaugh started the school out of his desire to repay a kindness extended to him by two individuals who had helped him achieve his educational goals when he was a young man. Louisville Tech's main academic programs include associate degrees in computer-aided design and drafting (CADD), computer engineering technology, and marine mechanics technology.

In 1993 the School of Fashion Merchandising and Design at Spencerian College and the interior design program at Louisville Tech merged to form a new division of Louisville Tech called the College of Merchandising and Design (CMD). This program now encompasses three creative disciplines: fashion merchandising, fashion design, and interior design.

Situated in a suburban area, the main campus for Louisville Tech and CMD includes 28,000 square feet of classrooms, labs, studios, and service areas, featuring industrial-quality equipment. The school's marine mechanics technology program is housed nearby in a separate facility.

Graduate Success and National Honors

The variety of programs available in the Sullivan system reflects a continuous effort to adapt to the changing economy and teach skills required for career success. At Sullivan College, students can receive diplomas in fields ranging from paralegal studies to computer science to professional nanny. The college's success in adapting to new career needs is measured by a 97 percent employment success rate for its graduates.

Sullivan's main campus provides a variety of technologically advanced training equipment. For example, travel and tourism students actually learn on American Airlines' SABRE computerized travel reservations system. Sullivan was one of only five colleges and universities chosen nationwide in 1994 to receive a Microsoft Education Development Grant for the improvement of computer education.

Many of the school's degree programs have been recognized nationally. For example, Sullivan's National Center for Hospitality Studies includes a renowned culinary arts program and offers associate degrees in culinary arts as well

as baking and pastry arts—one of the few such programs in the country that are accredited by the American Culinary Federation.

In 1993 chef instructor and master pastry chef Walter Rhea became the first American-born chef and educator ever to receive the American Culinary Association's Chef Professionalism Award. Rhea and other instructors have earned gold medals at the International Culinary Olympics, while Sullivan students have averaged more than 10 awards a year in culinary salon competitions sponsored by the American Culinary Federation.

Expanding Service for the Business Community

The Sullivan Colleges System established a new division in

1995: The Center for Business and Corporate Training. This division offers career training and continuing education on-site at participating businesses as well as on any of the system's six campuses. The focus of the program is the flexibility of its services—from upgrading employees' computer skills to helping a firm implement broad-based structural changes.

"The Center for Business and Corporate Training launches a whole new era of service and training for businesses and industries in the Kentuckiana market," says Thomas Davisson, vice president for school operations. "It's a logical step for an educational system committed to fulfilling the educational needs of Louisville's business community."

SULLIVAN COLLEGE'S NATIONAL CENTER FOR HOSPITALITY STUDIES INCLUDES A RENOWNED CULINARY ARTS PROGRAM—ONE OF THE FEW SUCH PROGRAMS IN THE COUNTRY THAT ARE ACCREDITED BY THE AMERICAN CULINARY FEDERATION—AND OFFERS ASSOCIATE DEGREES IN CULINARY ARTS, BAKING AND PASTRY ARTS, PROFESSIONAL CATERING, HOTEL/RESTAURANT MANAGEMENT, AND TRAVEL AND TOURISM.

AIRGUARD INDUSTRIES, INC.

IT IS PRESENT 24 HOURS A DAY, 365 DAYS A YEAR, MAKING LIFE possible, yet few individuals give it much thought. "It" is air, something many people take for granted—but not the employees of Louisville's Airguard Industries, one of the world's foremost producers and distributors of air filtration products. ♦ Wherever air is moved or conditioned—in homes, factories, hospitals, office buildings, schools, banks, and a host of

other applications—Airguard is present. Airguard is a subsidiary of CLARCOR Inc., a Rockford, Illinois-based manufacturer and distributor of mobile, industrial, and environmental filtration products and consumer packaging goods with more than $270 million in total annual sales.

Airguard has manufacturing facilities in Jeffersontown, Kentucky; New Albany, Indiana; Dallas, Texas; and Corona, California; with licensees in Toronto, Canada; Cairo, Egypt; and Riyadh, Saudi Arabia. More than 500 distributors worldwide carry Airguard products.

Originally formed to fill a void in the availability of aftermarket products to the HVAC industry, Airguard now devotes a growing portion of its production to original equipment manufacturers who in-

stall Airguard products within their own equipment. Additionally, in 1983 Airguard entered the new construction market, supplying air filter housings, equipment, and hardware for new buildings and modifications of existing systems.

Diversification notwithstanding, Airguard remains fundamentally true to its original concept, the manufacture and worldwide distribution of air filtration products, serving every facet of the HVAC aftermarket.

Leadership Role

Airguard's product line is second to none in the industry for total capability. Disposable filters, permanent filters, extended surface filters, high-efficiency particulate air (HEPA) filters, and dust collector cartridges are just a few of the many products Airguard manu-

factures. Whatever type of filtration equipment is installed, Airguard can provide a direct replacement or recommend alternatives for improved air cleaning efficiency, lower cost, or longer service life.

In addition to providing direct replacements, Airguard is continually developing innovative new products that lead the industry in design and performance. This philosophy is summed up in the company's slogan, "The industry looks to Airguard for leadership in air filtration technology."

Evidence of Airguard's product innovation is demonstrated in its response to the heightened market interest in improved indoor air quality. As the need to expand product capability beyond traditional particulate filtration became apparent, Airguard introduced the Vari-Pure high-capacity extended surface activated carbon filter to remove odors and gases.

Another example of industry leadership is antimicrobial treated products that inhibit growth of bacteria, fungi, mold, and mildew on the filters. Airguard's Bio-Pure filters are highly effective at preventing microbial growth on contact. This eliminates the filters as a source of contamination in a building.

Cleaning the President's Air

Airguard's products are installed in locations from the White House, to NASA, to Hyatt Hotels, to the Sears Tower. There is an Airguard product to meet every need, whether it be commercial, industrial, institutional, or residential. The company's factory-trained personnel will

THE EXPORT DEPARTMENT'S STAFF—(LEFT TO RIGHT) CHARLES ROGALINSKI, BOB SCHUTZ, BILL WALKER, MICHELE BEAMS, KATHLEEN MCDOUGALL, AND CHRISTY ROBINSON—DISCUSSES CUSTOMER REQUIREMENTS FOR A LARGE ORDER FOR CARTRIDGE DUST COLLECTORS.

conduct a comprehensive survey of the air-handling systems of any building to determine the requirements of each one and recommend the appropriate filter, based on the customer's specifications for efficiency, service life, labor, and other factors.

Backed by a program of strict quality control, enhanced by continuous sophisticated research and development, Airguard products are manufactured to rigid specifications using only the highest-quality components. The company's worldwide distribution network assures prompt delivery and its Quick Ship Plan offers rush service and reduces downtime in emergency situations.

Airguard's product line has been methodically augmented and broadened over the course of its more than 30-year history. Today, the company is universally recognized as having the most comprehensive product offering in the industry, including replacement filters for virtually every application, regardless of the manufacturer of the original equipment.

From Modest Beginnings to Industry Trendsetter

Airguard was founded in Louisville in 1964 with two employees. The fledgling company was principally a distributor of air filtration aftermarket products. In 1968 Airguard began manufacturing its own line of air filter products. From these mod-

est beginnings, the company has grown to become a full-line manufacturer of products for the HVAC aftermarket. The company's Quality Control Program, coupled with innovative research and development, assures consistent, top level performance. The distribution network, with representatives in every major city in the world, makes Airguard products available anywhere, anytime.

"Probably the key ingredient to our success has been the dedication of many long-term employees, some of whom have been with us almost since the beginning," proudly notes

Bill Walker, Airguard president. "We would not be where we are today if it were not for their commitment and leadership."

Airguard still occupies the site of the original two-employee office in Louisville. On that site today stands a modern complex housing the general headquarters and distribution operations for Kentucky and southern Indiana. Although Airguard looks back with pride on more than a quarter century of steady, consistent growth, it also looks forward with confidence to continued progress in the years to come.

THE MANUFACTURING FACILITY IN JEFFERSONTOWN, KENTUCKY, WAS RECENTLY EXPANDED TO 108,000 SQUARE FEET (ABOVE).

THE NEWEST DEVELOPMENT IN HIGH-EFFICIENCY FILTER MEDIA IS IN THE MICROFINE DUAL-LAYER SYNTHETIC FIBERS USED IN THE PRODUCTION OF VARI-PAK MODEL S FILTERS (BELOW LEFT).

BIO-PURE™ ANTIMICROBIAL-TREATED FILTERS HELP IMPROVE INDOOR AIR QUALITY BY INHIBITING GROWTH OF MICROORGANISMS ON THE FILTER (BELOW).

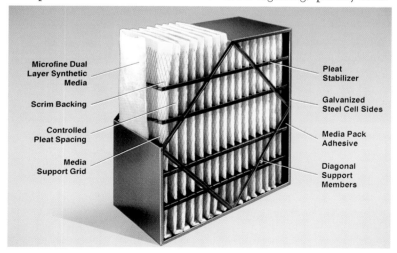

Microfine Dual Layer Synthetic Media

Scrim Backing

Controlled Pleat Spacing

Media Support Grid

Pleat Stabilizer

Galvanized Steel Cell Sides

Media Pack Adhesive

Diagonal Support Members

ROVIDIAN CORPORATION IS A LEADING PROVIDER OF consumer financial services, including life insurance, consumer credit and savings products, auto insurance, individual annuities, and group pension products. At least one of these products is sold in all 50 states. ◆ From its beginnings in 1969, Providian has grown to be a Fortune 500 company with more than $26

billion in assets and about 9,000 associates nationwide, working in four major operations: Providian Agency Group, Providian Direct Insurance, Providian Bancorp, and Providian Capital Management. More than 1,300 associates work in Louisville, the company's headquarters city.

While maintaining its roots as a life insurer, Providian has focused on its corporate strengths—results

PROVIDIAN CENTER, THE TALLEST BUILDING IN KENTUCKY, IS THE HEADQUARTERS OF PROVIDIAN CORPORATION.

orientation, a tradition of strong returns on investment, asset/liability management, targeting customers with unmet needs, and building long-term relationships with customers—to develop and offer a wider range of financial services. Individuals and families looking for protection, credit, and/or investment opportunities can turn to Providian confidently for all of these needs.

Providian Agency Group markets insurance and related services through a 2,600-member home service agent force. This business serves individuals and families throughout the southeast and mid-Atlantic states. Along with its agent sales activities, Agency Group also partners with third-party insurers to provide turnkey services.

Providian Direct Insurance sells life, automobile, and supplemental health insurance directly to individuals through telephone, television, and direct mail. PDI has evolved from being a mass marketer to a very successful target marketer, with core skills in market research and database management.

Providian Bancorp offers lending and deposit products nationwide through direct response marketing. These products include Visa® and Mastercard® credit cards, revolving lines of credit, home equity loans, and secured credit cards.

Providian Capital Management provides retirement savings products to individuals and groups of customers. Its products include fixed- and variable-rate annuities on the individual side and guaranteed investment contracts on the group side.

Sharing Expertise across Lines of Business

Although each of the four businesses has its own areas of expertise, one of the key goals of Providian's strategy is to market products and services across lines of business. "Increasingly, our businesses are operating across company lines to further our goals," says Chairman and CEO Irving W. Bailey II. "We aim to create opportunities that no one of our businesses can provide alone."

Until recently, most financial services were sold separately, or "unbundled." Banks provided credit; life insurance companies provided life insurance, and so on. Among the reasons were regulatory and technological barriers. Now, many of those barriers are falling.

Providian's vision is to take advantage of the new financial services arena to expand the range of services it provides to its customers. Until the mid-1990's, the company (formerly called Capital Holding Corporation) was known primarily as an acquirer of home service life insurance companies. "When we operated as a holding company, our businesses were managed independently," Bailey notes. "We are taking advantage of opportunities to share knowledge and experience among our businesses."

Now, Providian competes against banks, finance companies, mutual funds, and credit card providers—providing a single source for the products typically offered by those businesses.

Examples of successful cross-marketing abound. For instance, Providian Bancorp developed a product known as First Health Advantage[SM], a fee-based plan of discount medical services that was offered to credit card customers. When this same product was made available to Direct Insurance customers (as an addition to their insurance policies), the company made 45,000 sales in the first six months of this operation.

On another front, Providian Capital Management and Agency Group joined forces to provide new options for city, county, and state employee pension plans. "Our businesses share people, customers, capital, information, and technology," says Bailey.

Building Long-Term Relationships

The driving force behind Providian's overall marketing strategy is a careful focus on the company's targeted customers. In fact, Providian's goal is to support the financial goals of these customers through each stage of their lives. Therefore, the company seeks to build long-term relationships. For instance, young adults may need help obtaining credit as they begin their working lives or head to college. Later on, these same customers may need products such as life insurance or home-equity loans as they are starting families. Later still, annuities and other retirement planning services become vital.

As a result, many of Providian's customers have been served by the company for years, and a great number of their children become customers, too.

"Not only do we have products that serve our customers at various stages of their lives, we also can do business with them in the way they prefer," says Shailesh Mehta, Providian's chief operating officer. "For instance, some people like working with a qualified agent who'll come to their homes. Others are much more comfortable conducting business over the phone. We give both types of customers the

opportunity to obtain a range of services, no matter how they wish to access us."

While helping its customers reach their financial goals, Providian also works to support community goals in Louisville and other cities where it has a significant associate base. The company is a major contributor to community-enriching activities such as Metro United Way and Louisville's Fund for the Arts, and sponsors the Kentucky Derby Pegasus Parade and Project Safe Place.

Underscoring the importance of new information technology in

its own growth, Providian is also a supporter of efforts to create a well-trained workforce for the future. For instance, the company established a Challenge Grant in support of a $4.4 million fundraising campaign to upgrade the on-line information systems of the Louisville Free Public Library and its branches.

By improving the skills of those living in communities where it operates and improving financial opportunities for its customer base, Providian truly lives up to its name as a wide-ranging service provider.

WHILE MAINTAINING ITS ROOTS AS A LIFE INSURER, PROVIDIAN HAS FOCUSED ON ITS CORPORATEWIDE STRENGTHS TO DEVELOP AND OFFER A WIDER RANGE OF FINANCIAL SERVICES UNDER THE GUIDANCE OF PRESIDENT AND CHIEF OPERATING OFFICER SHAILESH MEHTA (LEFT) AND CHAIRMAN AND CHIEF EXECUTIVE OFFICER IRVING W. BAILEY II (BOTTOM RIGHT).

LOUISVILLE'S STEADY GROWTH AND OVERALL QUALITY OF LIFE ARE A product of an entrepreneurial spirit and the ongoing commitment by its business leaders to support the community. ◆ Thornton Oil Corporation is considered to be the city's premier privately held corporation holding the number-one position in Louisville's Metro 100 ranking for six of the 10 years the ranking has been measured.

Founded in 1971 by James H. Thornton and under the leadership of President and CEO Paul J. Perconti, Thornton Oil Corporation operates America's most innovative gasoline-convenience store outlets, which can be found throughout the Louisville landscape and more than 60 other cities in a six-state area.

The Entrepreneurial Spirit at Work

James Thornton started retailing gasoline in 1952 with a single station located across the river in New Albany, Indiana. Through his tenacity, integrity, high standards, and work ethic—and his undying commitment to bring value to the customer—he grew his investment to a chain of 150 Payless Stations. The Payless chain was bought by Ashland Oil Corporation in 1968. A true entrepreneur with a love of being a vital part of the community, Thornton started all over again three years later in 1971, establishing the company that bears his name: Thornton Oil Corporation.

For thousands of Louisvillian's and businesses around the Louisville area, Thornton's provides the highest-quality gasoline at a value and service level that leads the entire industry.

As always, the true measure of success is the ability to withstand the test of time, and with Thornton Oil Corporation servicing Louisville and many other cities for more than 25 years, the company passes that test with flying colors.

THORNTON OIL CORPORATION FOUNDER JAMES H. THORNTON (RIGHT) AND PRESIDENT AND CEO PAUL J. PERCONTI GUIDE THE COMPANY TODAY.

Doing a Little More, a Little Differently

From oil embargoes to snow storms, Thornton Oil Corporation has not only weathered adversity, but it appears to thrive on it.

The company's secret to success in the convenience business was brought about under the leadership of Perconti, who joined Thornton's in 1981. Perconti's strategic decision to embellish the company's existing sites and construct new ones that could offer a full line of convenience products proved to be a plan for success.

That decision had two beneficial consequences: First, it helped solidify a large customer base. And second, it provided a spring board for a strong and sustaining corporate growth.

But the secret to its success, employees agree, is much more than just expanded services. Everyone at Thornton's works hard to do a little more, a little differently, to make a difference to the consumer.

Thornton Oil was one of the first gasoline retailers to put canopies over its pumps. The company also added more space between pumps and extra lighting, which helped customers feel safe at night. Thornton's was one of the first in its industry to add automated teller machines (ATMs) to its locations and restaurants, as well as providing customers the ability to pay at the pump.

Thornton's is constantly working to improve the quality of the services and environment it provides to its customers. The company has long been recognized as a leader in the industry for its store designs and curb appeal.

Reaching to 100 Percent Plus

The daily success of Thornton Oil Corporation lies in the hands of its quality employees. Many ideas for improvement come from the employees who work in the individual stores.

Thornton's places such a strong emphasis on training its field personnel that it has launched a major quality initiative the company calls Restructure 2000. Employees in the field are the first point of contact for customers; they define what Thornton's is about. With Restructure 2000, Thornton Oil has empowered each employee to do what it takes to satisfy each customer.

Restructure 2000 is the largest investment of manpower and training in the company's history. "We're in a competitive environment that demands 100 percent excellence," Perconti says, "If 99.9 percent were acceptable, then in one year we would lose 60,000 customers, and our goal is not to lose any."

One doesn't need to look far for evidence that Thornton Oil employees believe in the 100 percent goal. When a snowstorm in January 1994 caused most Louisville-area businesses to close for up to four days, Thornton's

employees—including corporate staff—ventured out in four-wheel drive vehicles and kept the stores open. The company worked with its major dairy supplier—the dairy had an executive running the line—so Thornton's employees could pick up and distribute milk to the community when there was none to be found in the city.

A Continuing Critical Analysis

Thornton's plans to continue its aggressive expansion efforts toward the year 2000. The company operates in six states, primarily in the Midwest.

Thornton's is always looking for opportunities to provide innovative services within existing locations. Recently, the company became one of the first convenience retailers to co-brand with selected fast food leaders like McDonald's, Subway, Taco Bell, and Dunkin' Donuts. Through this arrangement, customers can stop at selected Thornton's locations, fill up on gas, purchase sundries, and get a quality meal from a fast food outlet located inside the store.

Perconti sums it up best when he says, "We are very thankful to our community for the enthusiastic support of our efforts, and we are most proud of our entire organization's undying commitment to 100 percent customer satisfaction." And serve it they do.

A THORNTON'S PROTOTYPE CONVENIENCE CENTER IN LOUISVILLE SETS THE PACE FOR CONVENIENCE IN AMERICA (LEFT).

THORNTON'S STATE-OF-THE-ART TRANSPORTATION FLEET CAN BE SEEN THROUGHOUT THE MIDWEST (BELOW).

THE WELLNESS INSTITUTE IS A PRIVATE, NOT-FOR-PROFIT organization whose mission is to promote healthy lifestyles by providing consultation, counseling, seminars, and other programs to individuals and organizations. Its current primary focus is on reducing the incidence of alcohol and other drug abuse and addiction by assisting individuals to be aware of and locate trained interventionists who

can help in arranging a responsible and caring personal family intervention.

A Lifetime of Caring

Institute Founder and President George "Doc" Perkins has made a career of caring for others. The recipient of a Ph.D. in metallurgical engineering from Purdue University and a one-time manager with Reynolds Metals Company, Perkins found he had a professional calling for helping people lead safer, fuller, and healthier lives.

Perkins left Reynolds in 1958 and has served the community through a series of jobs, ranging from executive director of Bellewood Presbyterian Home for Children and Commissioner of the Department of Child Welfare for the Commonwealth of Kentucky, to founder of the Human Development Company, a contract provider of Employee Assistance Programs (EAPs). Perkins' philosophy of wellness is based on emotional, mental, and spiritual well-being, as well as physical fitness.

Perkins started the Wellness Institute in 1971 as a vehicle to share his philosophy with others. "I began to see how many of our problems as a country are caused or made worse by alcohol and other forms of chemical dependence," Perkins says. "The current primary goal of the Wellness Institute is to assist the chemically dependent— and their loved ones—in working together to overcome these problems."

The Wellness Institute provides a wide range of educational and support services through a staff of five full- or part-time consultants. Services include client counseling, seminars, workshops, and volunteer training and development. In addition, the institute has a long-standing contract with the Western District of Kentucky of the U.S. District Court for counseling and a drug-screening program.

Importance of Personal Intervention

The Wellness Institute has worked with Rotary International and Hazelden Foundation to create a videotape program titled "Intervention: The Responsibility of Friends." In addition to documenting the huge financial and emotional costs of alcohol and other drug dependencies, the tape

features interviews with six individuals, each a member of a family that carried out a successful intervention. The bottom-line message is one of hope. Viewers who are personally affected by a friend or family member with an alcohol or other drug problem are encouraged to contact a trained interventionist and are told how to locate such a person.

Like other not-for-profit organizations, the Wellness Institute stretches its resources through joint activity with other community groups. In addition to Rotary International, the Institute has worked closely with the Wellness Forum, Kentucky Center for Health Education, Leadership Louisville, Leadership Kentucky, A.W.A.R.E. Coalition, and other entities.

Of all the Institute's diverse activities, the personal intervention program remains the most important. "Chemical dependence is the most costly problem in our society, both economically and emotionally. Personal intervention is a powerful tool for combating it. We need not wait for the friend or family member to hit the bottom of the barrel. We can help the person get into treatment now through a loving and caring confrontation," Perkins says. "The Wellness Institute can help you find a person to prepare the way for successful intervention."

INSTITUTE FOUNDER AND PRESIDENT GEORGE "DOC" PERKINS AT ROTARY INTERNATIONAL CONVENTION, JUNE 13, 1995, NICE, FRANCE (RIGHT).

GEORGE PERKINS' PHILOSOPHY OF WELLNESS IS BASED ON EMOTIONAL, MENTAL, AND SPIRITUAL WELL-BEING, AS WELL AS PHYSICAL FITNESS (BELOW).

WITH MORE THAN 30 YEARS IN THE HOTEL INDUSTRY, the Hyatt Corporation has established a worldwide reputation for excellence. The Hyatt Regency Louisville, the choice of thousands of guests annually, is certainly no exception. It offers all the warmth and refinement of fine Southern hospitality in the heart of a vibrant metropolis. ◆ For

more than 15 years, the Hyatt Regency Louisville has been the only premier chain hotel in the downtown area. Located across the street from the Commonwealth Convention Center, it plays host to hundreds of national and regional gatherings. The hotel is only minutes away from Louisville International Airport. Adjacent to a unique shopping attraction in the downtown area, the Galleria shopping mall, the hotel offers a number of guest amenities, including an indoor pool, hydrospa, tennis court, and health club.

A Commitment to Guests

The Hyatt Regency Louisville can boast of being the most updated hotel in the city. Completely equipped for the business traveler's needs, the hotel's features include voice mail, dataport access, iron and ironing board, and a coffee maker in each guest room. The Business Plan Floor offers guests an innovative concept in accommodations, designed specifically for the business traveler. The floor features free local calls, complimentary breakfast, personal workstations, in-room facsimile machines, and more.

"Our commitment to the business traveler and to keeping up with the latest technology makes us unique," explains Director of Sales Annette Kaplan. "Also, our people make a big difference. Our motto, 'Discover the people with the Hyatt Touch' applies to the quality of service our guests have come to expect from Hyatt Hotels."

But great service and convenient technology are not all the

Hyatt Regency Louisville has to offer. There are also 388 spacious guest rooms and suites (including Regency Club® and Gold Passport® accommodations), as well as more than 21,000 square feet of flexible function space that allows for gatherings of almost any size from 10 to 1,000. And, the hotel features an atrium cafe, a cozy sports bar, and a sidewalk cafe, plus a spectacular revolving rooftop restaurant featuring fine dining and a panoramic view of Louisville.

For guests who wish to explore the city's cultural attractions, the Hyatt Regency Louisville is within walking distance of the theater district, Kentucky Center for the Arts, and Louisville Gardens.

"Of course, we look forward to the Kentucky Derby every year. We're only a short distance to Churchill Downs. We play a large role in the success of the Derby each year and host several Derby Festival events," says Kaplan.

Continuous Attention to a First-Class Property

The Hyatt Regency Louisville is continuously refurbished and

upgraded. The hotel completed a $4.5 million renovation of its guest rooms in 1992 and updated the lobby and cafe in 1994. During 1995 the rooftop restaurant received a face-lift and a revised menu. The hotel's management understands that maintaining a first-class reputation requires constant attention.

What does the future hold for the Hyatt Regency Louisville? Kaplan says, "We're optimistic. More people are traveling to Louisville for business and pleasure. With airfares more affordable, occupancy is projected to increase. We think Louisville is a growing area, and we're ready to grow with it."

WHETHER MEETING IN ONE OF THE HYATT REGENCY LOUISVILLE'S CONFERENCE ROOMS OR DINING IN ITS ROOFTOP RESTAURANT, GUESTS ENCOUNTER TOP-QUALITY SERVICE.

Mention the Borden company and most people think about dairy products. But the company founded by Gail Borden back in 1857 is also a leading producer of chemical products—particularly adhesives. The link between dairy products and glue is found in an ingredient called casein, the principal protein in milk.

Casein was used to produce the first successful water-resistant wood glue. In 1899 Borden bought the Casein Manufacturing Company in Vermont, entering the chemical industry to become one of the top 25 chemical producers in the United States.

Louisville is the headquarters of Borden's North American Resins Group, part of the company's and most advanced resin plant, as well as one of the group's research and development facilities. Borden's operations in Louisville include the large operating plant and research facility, which are located near the Ohio River in the western part of the city, plus the headquarters staff offices for the resins group, located in downtown Louisville.

the unit's growth has been aided by a trend in construction toward using a wood construction panel product called oriented strand board, which uses more resin than traditional plywood. Plus, medium density fiberboard, a type of particle board bonded by Borden resins, has become increasingly popular for furniture and other interior woodworking purposes.

FROM ITS HEADQUARTERS IN LOUISVILLE, BORDEN MAINTAINS ITS WORLD LEADERSHIP BY SETTING INDUSTRY STANDARDS FOR QUALITY, TECHNOLOGY, AND CUSTOMER SERVICE.

© DAN DRY / DAN DRY & ASSOCIATES

Worldwide Packaging and Industrial Products Division. The resins group, which employs about 1,400 people, was formed in 1993 by a consolidation of three operating units: Forest Products, Foundry Products, and Industrial Products.

Louisville: A Place for Continued Growth

Although the North American Resins Group was consolidated in the 1990s, Borden has operated in Louisville since the early 1970s, making the city a logical choice to locate the group. Louisville is centrally located for both Borden's customers and its various resin group operations and is home to the company's largest

"We're the number one or two producer/seller for virtually all the markets and customers we serve," says Ed Krainer, vice president and group general manager. "We provide our customers with outstanding service and the best quality products . . . that's what we're about." Indeed, the 1990s have been a period of strong growth for each of the business units that make up Borden's North American Resins Group.

The Forest Products unit is the largest portion of the North American Resins Group, producing more than 3 billion pounds of adhesives for wood products such as plywood, particle board, and hardboard. Krainer explains that

The Foundry Products unit produces resin binders, resin-coated sand, and refractory coatings used in making many types of metal-casting cores and molds. Among the biggest users of these cores and molds are foundries that supply domestic automobile manufacturers, who use them for producing iron and aluminum castings.

The Industrial Products unit produces resins for the automotive, electronics, oil and gas, and aircraft industries. Among its chief products are resins used in producing acoustical insulation, brake linings, and oil filters for automotives; thermal insulation for homes; oil-field proppants; aircraft interior panels; and computer parts and laminates.

"One of our fastest-growing areas is in specialized products for the electronics industry," notes Michael George, vice president and director of operations for the resins group. "They're used in the production of circuit boards and silicon computer chips. They have to be very, very pure. It's a high-tech product."

The company's vision statement declares that Borden will maintain its world leadership in the markets it serves by setting the standard for quality, technology, and customer service. In fact, technology is one of the resins group's primary advantages. A good illustration is the resin product used in high-end electronic circuitry, which is shipped to customers in Europe and Japan, as well as the United States.

Watching the Six O'clock Position

"Our most important advantage," says Krainer, "is that we always try to look at our business from the customer's side. I don't see how you could stay where we are without doing that."

Constant improvement is a constant concern of Krainer and his management team. One of his favorite pieces of advice is "Don't forget to watch your six o'clock position." The advice, which he learned from a friend who was a military pilot, refers to the need to check directly behind you (the six o'clock position) to make sure you're not being chased and to avoid becoming too complacent.

To promote superior service and constant improvements, the North American Resins Group is organized into cross-functional teams—some of which cross not only operating units but also national borders. For example, an international team recently worked on overhauling the group's management information system.

Many Borden teams start out at the business-planning level, where they set goals and plan for the future. More often than not, these planning teams then spin off one or more project teams (also cross-functional) that actually implement the new objectives.

"All of our associates are trained in the team process," says Krainer. "While we recognize the importance of individual efforts, we also believe good teamwork can lead to even greater accomplishments."

With good teamwork, Borden and its Louisville-based North American operations hope to continue to stay in front of the competition while keeping an eye on the six o'clock position to continually improve.

TO PROMOTE SUPERIOR SERVICE AND CONSTANT IMPROVEMENTS, BORDEN'S NORTH AMERICAN RESINS GROUP IS ORGANIZED INTO CROSS-FUNCTIONAL TEAMS—SOME OF WHICH CROSS NOT ONLY OPERATING UNITS BUT ALSO NATIONAL BORDERS.

© DAN DRY/DAN DRY & ASSOCIATES

© DAN DRY/DAN DRY & ASSOCIATES

THE HURSTBOURNE HOTEL AND CONFERENCE CENTER

THE HURSTBOURNE HOTEL AND CONFERENCE CENTER, LOUISVILLE'S third-largest freestanding convention facility, is the largest hotel in the city's prestigious East End. With 399 guest rooms—52 of which are suites—and more than 50,000 square feet of self-contained, unobstructed meeting and event space, the Hurstbourne Hotel and Conference Center serves as an economic anchor for the eastern sector of the

Louisville metropolitan area.

The property's position within the local economy has been instrumental in coordinating two community initiatives—the Hurstbourne Association Business Connection and the East End Shuttle municipal bus service—that together streamline commerce and enhance the experience of visitors to the city's Hurstbourne area.

Louisville's Hurstbourne Association Business Connection is a merchant association that joins the hotel and convention center with other hotels, restaurants, and a variety of service providers in the Hurstbourne area. The merchant association offers amenities and services for the many convention-going visitors who flock annually through Kentucky's largest city, named one of the top 13 convention destinations in the country by the American Society of Association Executives.

In addition to helping form Louisville's Hurstbourne Association Business Connection, the hotel and conference center worked with the city's municipal transportation provider, TARC (Transit Author-

ity of River City), to establish the East End Shuttle, which assists workers in the Hurstbourne and East End areas in reaching their job sites from various parts of the city. More than 200 of those workers are Hurstbourne Hotel and Conference Center associates. The location of the hotel and conference center in Louisville's East End offers quick access to the city's interstate highway system, making it simple to get around the metropolitan area and attend convention-related events and activities. From the Hurstbourne locale, guests also find it easy to take advantage of many local and regional attractions, such as Churchill Downs—famous home of the Kentucky Derby—and Keeneland Race Track, just 75 minutes east in Lexington.

High-Tech Hospitality
For convention-goers ranging from hosts to vendors to visitors, the Hurstbourne Hotel and Con-

ference Center offers a flexible, modern environment for meeting and networking. An array of options are available for different-sized groups with varying technology needs. Within the 50,000 square feet of meeting space, there are 14 column-free rooms with seating capacities ranging from 18 to 2,500 people. Assistance with arrangements for equipment and facilities is available to planners and speakers through an on-site convention services manager as well as in-house experts on audio-visual presentations.

Of special note is the enormous Grande Belle Hall, which, with 22,000 square feet of open space, is one of the largest facilities of its kind in the city. The room can accommodate theater-style seating as well as more than 100 eight-foot by 10-foot exhibit booths. The Julia Belle Hall seats more than 500, offering space suited for dinners,

A SPECIAL FEATURE OF THE HURSTBOURNE HOTEL & CONFERENCE CENTER IS ITS 16,800-SQUARE-FOOT TROPIDOME, OFFERING YEAR-ROUND USE OF TWO FULLY ENCLOSED SWIMMING POOLS, A GAMES ARCADE, A JACUZZI, A DRY SAUNA, AND AN EXERCISE FACILITY (RIGHT).

OF SPECIAL NOTE AT THE HURSTBOURNE IS THE ENORMOUS GRANDE BELLE HALL, WHICH—WITH 22,000 SQUARE FEET OF OPEN SPACE—IS ONE OF THE LARGEST FACILITIES OF ITS KIND IN THE CITY (BELOW).

wedding receptions, or social events. Two outdoor courtyards are also available for reservation.

The 52 suites at the Hurstbourne Hotel and Conference Center include 10 spacious hospitality parlors, 37 two-room club suites, and five Jacuzzi suites. All rooms offer a full cable package with complimentary HBO and ESPN, Spectradyne featuring first-run pay movies, room service, and individual temperature controls.

A special feature of the Hurstbourne Hotel and Conference Center is its 16,800-square-foot Tropidome, offering year-round use of two fully enclosed swimming pools, a games arcade, a Jacuzzi, a dry sauna, and an exercise facility. Guests may enjoy many on-site conveniences, including dining at Cristy's, the hotel's on-site restaurant; Cristy's Bakery; Legends Lounge, offering nightly live entertainment; the Comedy Club; beauty and barber shops; and a gift shop.

Year-Round Caring

A significant contributor to local commerce, the Hurstbourne Hotel and Conference Center also gets involved in activities that benefit the community. Associates form teams to participate annually in Louisville's Dare to Care campaign, gathering food for the city's homeless and others in need. In 1994 Hurstbourne associates ran the United We Stand Against Hunger campaign to raise more than 50,000 pounds of food within a two-week period.

The hotel and conference center is also involved in activities benefiting the Crusade for Children, as well as Dare to Care's Kids' Cafe program, which provides holiday goodies for children. Hurstbourne management makes a special point of ensuring that its contribution to Kids' Cafe benefits children throughout the entire year, not just during the December holiday season.

Positive Impact

Owned by the Atlanta-based Impac Hotel Group, the Hurstbourne Hotel and Conference Center is an exemplar of Impac's unyielding dedication to customer satisfaction. The Hurstbourne organization consistently focuses on the most basic premise in the hotel industry: total guest satisfaction. Companywide, all Impac hotel associates are fully empowered to carry out the organization's entrepreneurial credo: "If a guest is not completely satisfied with any particular portion of their room, service, meal, meeting, function, or any other part of our facility, that specific portion of their experience will unconditionally be complimentary." All associates are authorized to resolve a guest's dissatisfaction on the spot.

Louisville's Hurstbourne Hotel and Conference Center is one of 20 properties in the Impac portfolio. While Impac counts other convention hotels among its properties, Hurstbourne is the only conference center facility in the eight states in which Impac has a presence.

Whether serving as an economic anchor for the community or providing outstanding service to its patrons, the Hurstbourne Hotel and Conference Center will continue to be a vital contributor to the Louisville area.

THE 52 SUITES AT THE HURSTBOURNE HOTEL & CONFERENCE CENTER INCLUDE 10 SPACIOUS HOSPITALITY PARLORS, 37 TWO-ROOM CLUB SUITES, AND FIVE JACUZZI SUITES.

POWER GRAPHICS, INC.

ESTABLISHED IN 1976 AS A GRAPHIC DESIGN FIRM, POWER Graphics has evolved into one of the premier marketing and communications companies in the Midwest. Located on Commonwealth Drive in the east end of Louisville, Power has assembled a group of talented and energetic people who work as a team to find solutions, ideas that work in the marketplace, for

their clients. The company specializes in helping businesses target and communicate effectively with their markets.

The Power team consists of more than 70 skilled individuals, working together to create distinctive and effective design solutions. The 25,000-square-foot Louisville facility houses a wide array of services, from marketing and design to in-house copywriting and photography.

POWER GRAPHICS COUNTS AMONG ITS MANY CLIENTS WATERFRONT DEVELOPMENT CORPORATION, DEVELOPERS OF LOUISVILLE'S WATERFRONT PARK.

The primary philosophy of Power lies in the belief that there is nothing so powerful as the right idea, properly executed. The objective is to communicate these ideas by using the creative process to deliver the message in an arresting and persuasive way. Power carefully oversees each stage in the process, developing the perfect blend of art and science.

The creative process begins with account management teams who provide creative direction based on a sound understanding of marketing objectives and strategies. Account managers work with

art directors, designers, photographers, electronic imaging specialists, and production artists to constantly monitor the progress of jobs. Attention to detail in design, administration, and technical accuracy is never compromised.

Comprehensive services include production of traditional marketing and sales materials, as well as electronic media such as CD-ROM-based presentations and World Wide Web site development and administration. Photography, food styling, set construction, and architectural rendering are also integral parts of Power service.

Over the past four years Power has made significant investments, not only to compete more efficiently, but also to set the standard for merchandising material design. Human resources are continually enhanced and expanded, with ongoing training and development added to further enhance skill levels. Ongoing capital investments in computer hardware and software have strengthened Power's ability to produce the highest-quality materials by the most effective and efficient means possible.

Power Photography perceives art as the fusion of technology and creativity. Its technicians are adept in the many skills required for a variety of formats and techniques, including digital photography and file management. Because photography is such an essential element in the creative service, Power has included food styling and set construction as in-house services.

Maintaining the integrity of the approved design concept during the photographic execution is essential to effective communication. A skilled photography staff and stylist/home economist work with art directors to ensure each photograph represents the product in accordance with the marketing objectives. This turnkey approach is not only more efficient, but also provides more creative control.

The Architectural Marketing division of Power is a highly specialized graphics service, designed to assist architects and real estate developers in marketing commercial/retail developments. A staff of architectural artists provides detailed renderings for presentations—assuring that each project reflects the innovation of the design. This internationally recognized team is called upon by many of today's most influential and progressive architects and developers to create a wide range of materials, from informational brochures to retail advertising/marketing programs.

Power has won the trust of its clients through its objectivity, broad creative perspective, and ability to efficiently coordinate and direct a number of disciplines on their behalf. Power's approach has a special relevance in today's marketplace, as companies depend more and more on a strong, consistent visual identity for effective marketing results.

UNITED CATALYSTS INC.

UNITED CATALYSTS INC. (UCI) IS AN AFFILIATED COMPANY OF Süd-Chemie AG of Munich, Germany, which began as a manufacturer of specialty catalysts for the fertilizer, chemical, and petroleum-refining industries. Süd-Chemie was incorporated in December 1857 and traces its beginnings to the famed German scientist Justus von Liebig, who developed the formula for superphosphate fertilizers. Süd-Chemie began to manufacture superphosphate and sulfuric acid in 1860.

United Catalysts was formed in Louisville in 1977 by Süd-Chemie AG through the merger of Girdler Chemical, Inc. and Catalysts and Chemicals Inc. Girdler Chemical's history in Louisville goes back to the mid-1940s as Girdler Engineering Co., and Catalysts and Chemicals started operations in Louisville in 1957. Today, there are four major divisions within UCI—employing roughly 900 people— which include the Catalysts Division, Rheological Division, Desiccants Division, and Clay and Minerals Division. The products that UCI supplies touch virtually everyone, from the food people eat to the clothes they wear and the homes they live in.

Over the years, United Catalysts Inc. has diversified into other fields to become, in addition to its position in the catalysts field, a leading producer of rheological additives, desiccants, and industrial minerals.

Catalyzing the World

UCI's Catalysts Division produces heterogeneous catalysts for the fertilizer, petroleum, and chemical industries, and, more recently, emission control catalysts for protecting the environment. Catalysts accelerate chemical reactions, creating a chemical change in milliseconds that ordinarily might take years. Unconsumed by the reaction, catalysts work for years before requiring replacement.

Research and development on many of the major commercial catalytic applications are performed by this group, along with the associated engineering designs and field technical services. Catalyst manufacturing is the original activity of United Catalysts, and two manufacturing plants and laboratories are located in Louisville. The city also serves as headquarters for a group of companies that includes the affiliates Catalysts and Chemicals

CATALYST MANUFACTURING IS UNITED CATALYSTS INC.'S ORIGINAL ACTIVITY, WITH THREE UCI MANUFACTURING PLANTS AND LABORATORIES LOCATED IN LOUISVILLE.

Inc., Far East, which is located in Tokyo, Japan, and United Catalysts India Inc., located in New Delhi, India.

A strong capability in research and development, coupled with extensive testing facilities, makes United Catalysts a complete and innovative catalyst supplier. Aside from producing its own catalysts, UCI also manufactures proprietary catalysts for many chemical manufacturers. These are developed in the laboratories of the various companies and require manufacturing to precise specifications.

Expanding Presence

In 1990 UCI acquired the Houdry catalyst business from Air Products and Chemicals in Allentown, Pennsylvania, and built a modern, state-of-the-art manufacturing plant in Louisville, which began operation in 1993. The Houdry Division manufactures proprietary chrome-alumina catalysts in Louisville for worldwide sale.

Houdry's Catofin® and Catadiene® catalysts are used for the dehydrogenation of propane and butanes in the production of propylene, isobutylene, and butadiene.

Propylene's major use is for the production of polypropylene plastic. Polypropylene is widely used to produce many consumer products such as olefin composite, appliance parts, and packaging. The major use of isobutylene is to make MTBE— a gasoline additive that greatly reduces air pollution. The manufacture of tires and various high-strength plastic items utilizes butadiene.

Pyrotol® and Detol® catalysts manufactured by Houdry are used to produce high-purity benzene by hydrodealkylation of pyrolysis gasoline and toluene. Houdry's Litol® catalyst is used to upgrade coke oven light oils.

In 1992 UCI acquired Prototech, a small company in Massachusetts that produces high-quality environmental control catalysts. These catalysts are both precious and base metal in composition, and are available in pellet and monolith form. They serve a wide range of clean-air control markets, including paint booths, printing plants, can coating, metal decorating, furniture manufacture, and soil remediation. In addition to catalysts, Prototech also provides testing and cleaning/rejuvenation services.

Other applications for Prototech catalysts include wood stoves, cooking ovens, and fast-food restaurants. Automotive off-road vehicles and auto-convertor retrofits benefit from catalytic technology. Prototech catalysts also are employed to control gaseous emissions from stationary engines, turbines, package boilers, and petrochemical plants.

A Flow of Great Products

Süd-Chemie AG expanded its rheological business into the Western Hemisphere in 1979 with the exporting of Tixogel® organoclay products from its plant in Germany. The Tixogel plant in Louisville was opened in late 1980.

In April 1984, with the acquisition of the York Castor Oil Company in New Jersey, the Rheological Division more than doubled its product line. The acquisition was a strategic move in ensuring the growth of the division, as these castor-based products complement the Tixogel organoclay thixotropes.

In 1991 the Rheological Division introduced a new generation of organoclays referred to as the Maximum Performance or "MP" line of products. This new technology represents the highest-performance and most efficient organoclays available in the world today.

In mid-1993 Süd-Chemie restructured the corporation to form worldwide business units. Today, Süd-Chemie Rheologicals is headquartered in Louisville, offering a single high standard

of quality and service throughout the world.

The technical service laboratories in Louisville and Moosburg, Germany, solve cutting-edge technical problems with cutting-edge product solutions and create new opportunities for success with customers. The Rheological Research and Development Group works continuously on developing new technology and products for the industries it serves.

A STRONG CAPABILITY IN RESEARCH AND DEVELOPMENT, COUPLED WITH EXTENSIVE TESTING FACILITIES, MAKES UNITED CATALYSTS INC. A COMPLETE AND INNOVATIVE CATALYST SUPPLIER.

Dryly Innovative

In the Desiccants Business Unit, United Desiccants mines and packages desiccants, including montmorillonite clay, activated carbon, silica gel, and molecular sieve. Desiccants are drying agents, and they are used to protect machinery, electronics, food, pharmaceuticals, military equipment, and other packaged products from moisture damage. UCI's packaged desiccants will

protect the contents of a sealed container until it is opened.

In 1983 United Catalysts built a plant in Belen, New Mexico, for the processing and bagging of a high grade of activated montmorillonite clay from the United Desiccants' mine in Arizona. In 1985 UCI acquired the N.T. Gates Co., which has been a supplier of desiccants to the pharmaceutical, military, textile, and food industries since its founding in 1952. Manufacturing for United Desiccants and N.T. Gates has been consolidated at the New Mexico plant site.

In December 1994 the Desiccants Business Unit completed construction of a new plant for Humidial Corporation in Colton, California. Humidial Corporation manufactures color-change chemical humidity indicator cards and plugs. The indicators and plugs allow visual inspection of the condition of a sealed package by readily detecting any change in relative humidity on an easy-to-read, color-change element.

Bringing New Resources to Light

The Clay and Minerals Division is home to the Albion Kaolin Company, which is located in Hephzibah, Georgia. The oldest, continuously operating kaolin clay mine in the United States, Albion Kaolin extracts and produces high-purity kaolin clays for the paper, rubber, plastics, ceramic, refractory, fiberglass, chemical, and agricultural industries.

Albion Kaolin products are the result of both airfloat and slurry processing. The airfloated products are high-purity, low-moisture kaolin powders that have undergone flash drying, roller-mill pulverizing, degritting, and final purification by passing through air-classification systems. Slurry items are produced by multiple wet-screening, selective blending, and chemical additions. All kaolin products are guaranteed to give consistent performance. In addition to production, the company

coordinates technical service, quality control, and product development for the division.

Zeochem, a joint venture of United Catalysts and Chemische Fabrik Uetikon of Switzerland, produces synthetic zeolites for dehydration, chemical processing, and catalytic application.

Zeochem was formed in 1980 to manufacture and market molecular sieves as absorbents and catalyst supports for the chemical industries in the United States, other parts of the Western Hemisphere, and the Orient. Products made in the Zeochem plant—which is located adjacent to the United Catalysts production facility in Louisville—are used in petroleum and petrochemical processing, sealed insulating glass, paint and coatings, ethanol production, refrigeration, air drying and purification, and air brakes.

At UCI, products are manufactured in both continuous and batch operations. Key steps in these operations are controlled to ensure uniformity of product in a variety of configurations, including pellets, spheres, raschig rings, and tablets. To further assure uniformity, all products are made to fixed formulations and procedures monitored by continuous process control. The techniques of manufacture are critical, and considerable emphasis is placed on process and quality control tests.

SPC and ISO Spell Quality

All divisions of UCI are incorporating statistical process control (SPC) programs into areas of manufacturing and service operations. United Catalysts had a tremendously successful pilot SPC program in 1987, whereby a custom catalyst was manufactured in Louisville for a major chemical producer using a process that was statistically controlled. SPC provides all of UCI's employees with the knowledge and statistical tools to assist in the manufacture of quality products and services that meet a customer's requirements each and every time.

Expanding on the SPC programs, United Catalysts has implemented two additional management initiatives. In March 1995 UCI South Plant received International Organization for Standardization (ISO) 9001 certification for all product lines. In January the West Catalyst Plant began the certification process, and in June 1995 it was joined by Houdry Catalyst. By 1997 all Louisville-based catalyst plants will be under the same ISO 9001 quality management system. In addition, the West Catalyst Plant is continuing the conversion from line and staff management to self-directed work teams. With this team approach comes employee empowerment coupled with the

structure and discipline of continuous improvement under ISO 9001. The conversion will eventually become the business management system for all the Louisville-based plants.

UCI welcomes the challenge of using the quality process for the development of new products to meet the expanding needs of its customers.

Progress and Stewardship

United Catalysts is a member of the Chemical Manufacturers Association (CMA). In keeping with CMA's requirements, United Catalysts implemented its Responsible Care® program in 1991. The purpose of the program is the enhancement of community awareness, improved employee safety and health, and

a cleaner environment. This is accomplished through six management practice codes: community awareness and emergency response, process safety, distribution, pollution prevention, employee safety and health, and product stewardship.

Growth in all divisions— Catalysts, Rheological, Desiccants, and Clay and Minerals, as well as the Zeochem joint venture—will catalyze UCI into keeping pace with the rapid developments in its industry, and will help the company transform those developments into the products that mean so much to so many. United Catalysts' commitment to continuous improvement applies as much to being a good corporate neighbor as it does to being a world leader in chemical engineering products.

OVER THE YEARS, UNITED CATALYSTS INC. HAS DIVERSIFIED INTO OTHER FIELDS TO BECOME, IN ADDITION TO ITS POSITION IN THE CATALYSTS FIELD, A LEADING PRODUCER OF RHEOLOGICAL ADDITIVES, DESICCANTS, AND INDUSTRIAL MINERALS.

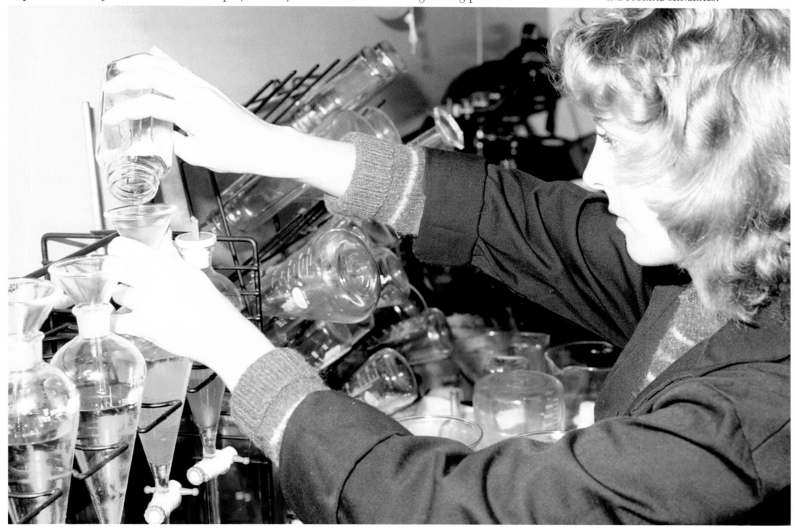

GREATER LOUISVILLE ECONOMIC DEVELOPMENT PARTNERSHIP

THROUGHOUT THE 1990S GREATER LOUISVILLE HAS BEEN ONE OF America's most successful urban economies. From 1990 to 1994 the metropolitan area of just under a million people added more than 58,000 new jobs, $3 billion in payroll growth, and well over $2.5 billion in new business investment—a record few communities its size can match. ◆ But Louisville wasn't always so fortunate. In the early 1980s the area

lost 34,000 manufacturing jobs, suffered through double-digit unemployment, and saw its population decline. Louisville was a classic rust-belt city, slowly dying.

What caused the dramatic turnaround? One key has been a concentrated, coordinated effort to diversify Louisville's economy by recruiting new business to the region. And the organization responsible for that recruitment is the Greater Louisville Economic Development Partnership.

The seeds for the Partnership were planted in 1987, when local governmental and business launched a $10 million fund-raising campaign to bolster the region's competitive strength, after a study showed that Louisville lagged far behind other cities in economic development and business attraction. By late 1988 the Partnership was formed.

On-Target Business Attraction

The Partnership's mission is to attract new jobs and investments to Greater Louisville from outside the region. The Partnership also

CLOCKWISE FROM RIGHT: PARTNERSHIP STAFF PROVIDES A MULTITUDE OF SERVICES, INCLUDING CONFIDENTIAL SITE-SELECTION ASSISTANCE AND DETAILED ECONOMIC RESEARCH.

SEARS TELESERVICE CENTER AND CREDIT CENTRAL OPERATIONS EMPLOY A TOTAL OF 2,300 PEOPLE IN LOUISVILLE.

THE PARTNERSHIP HELPED ATTRACT AMGEN'S $12 MILLION, STATE-OF-THE-ART DISTRIBUTION CENTER TO LOUISVILLE.

▼▲ © DAN DRY / DAN DRY & ASSOCIATES

plays a central role in supporting and coordinating local economic growth initiatives.

Why is this kind of activity important? "The fact is, every locale in America is competing for employment," says Brad Richardson, Partnership president. "Without a game plan to attract industry to the region, Louisville would be at a grave disadvantage, especially when competing against cities like Cincinnati, Indianapolis, Atlanta, Denver, and Nashville. The Partnership is the organization that provides Louisville with that game plan."

The game plan has proved successful. From 1991 through 1994 the area's economy grew by 9 percent, according to a study by the Bureau of Economic Research at the University of Louisville. (The nation's growth for the same period was 5.3 percent.) In 1994 alone, the regional economy gained 18,000 jobs and set an all-time employment record of nearly 526,000 jobs.

The Partnership was a major force in these gains. In its first seven years, it helped recruit more than 100 companies to Greater Louisville, resulting in more than 16,000

new jobs (more than 10,000 in direct employment and the balance in spin-off positions). These new positions accounted for $250 million in direct payroll and more than $350 million in total payroll growth.

Investors judge value by scrutinizing the return on investment. Viewed from this perspective, the Partnership's numbers are particularly impressive. With a total outlay of about $8 million through 1994, the Partnership brought in an annual yield of $234 million in new payroll. The average cost per job attracted by the Partnership works out to about $800—a bargain by any standard.

Selling Louisville to the World

The Partnership employs a professional staff of 10 people. Basically, the organization works in two areas—communications and business attraction.

The mission of the communications staff is to build a stronger, more positive image of Louisville nationally through marketing materials, advertising, direct mail, and public relations campaigns. The Partnership even developed an

FORD'S KENTUCKY TRUCK PLANT, WHICH MANUFACTURES ALL OF THE COMPANY'S MEDIUM- AND HEAVY-DUTY TRUCKS IN NORTH AMERICA, BEGAN A $650 MILLION EXPANSION IN 1992 WITH PARTNERSHIP ASSISTANCE.

award-winning TV commercial that was aired during the national telecast of the Kentucky Derby in 1994 and 1995.

The second major area is business attraction. "We take a very proactive approach to recruiting businesses," Richardson says. "We don't wait for them to come to Louisville. We go out after them." In a typical year, Partnership representatives meet with more than 100 potential prospects in locations around the United States, Canada, and even Japan.

When prospects visit Louisville, the Partnership utilizes the city's most effective sales force: satisfied area businesses. Hometown firms give prospects a positive first-hand feel for Louisville's many advantages. Local companies have also teamed up with the Partnership to attract their suppliers to the region.

All this hard work has paid off: Since 1987, the Partnership has been instrumental in recruiting prime projects for sites around the region, such as Stride Rite's $35 million national distribution center; Sears Credit Central and Tele-

service Center, two facilities that together employ about 2,300; and Amgen's $12 million, biopharmaceutical distribution facility.

Community Commitment

In addition to recruiting businesses, the Partnership has been involved in a number of important community-development projects. "Our philosophy is that Greater Louisville is our product," says Richardson, "and an important part of our job is to improve the product."

Toward that end, the Partnership made major investments in a $530 million upgrading of Louisville International Airport, a $650 million expansion of a local Ford plant, and the Regional Economic Development Strategy, a farsighted

program for the enhancement of Louisville not simply as a place to do business, but as a total community. Addressing such critical areas as land use, transportation, education, workforce training, minority business development, and government relations, the Regional Economic Development Strategy provides a blueprint for a promising future.

The Greater Louisville Economic Development Partnership sees a bright future for the region. "We've come a long way in a short time, but we've barely tapped our potential," says Richardson. "The challenge that lies ahead is to continue generating good job opportunities while preserving our community's outstanding quality of life."

STRIDE RITE'S $35 MILLION NATIONAL DISTRIBUTION FACILITY OPENED IN 1993 AND EMPLOYS 250 WORKERS.

RUDENTIAL SERVICE BUREAU (PSB) PROVIDES CLIENTS FROM across the nation with a broad array of the latest in human resource and benefit services from its Louisville headquarters. As part of The Prudential, the largest insurance company in North America and one of the most substantial financial organizations in the world, PSB is positioned to play a vital role in the rapidly changing benefits

industry of the 1990s and beyond.

PSB, founded in 1987, represents one of The Prudential's most recent success stories in a long history of innovation in insurance and financial services. Anticipating a future trend in the outsourcing of employee benefits, The Prudential opened PSB in Louisville (with satellite offices in other cities) to offer employers a cost-effective alternative to handling the full load of benefits and human resource administration themselves.

A Leading Source for Outsourcing

"In today's ultracompetitive environment, companies face every conceivable challenge," says Sandy Wadsworth, director of marketing. "PSB can help by tackling important but resource-consuming administrative functions. That leaves the employer with more time to concentrate on the core mission of his or

her organization."

Indeed, the outsourcing of benefits administration can increase an organization's competitiveness. Human resource personnel are able to focus on more pressing needs when cost-center functions are turned over to PSB specialists. Management enjoys the availability of new, freed-up resources. And, employee

morale is strengthened through a wider range of customized benefit options.

PSB offers a complete line of benefits outsourcing services. These include enrollments, internal communication services, administration of flexible benefit plans (cafeteria plans), life insurance record keeping, customer-service support, COBRA administration and individual billing services, carrier and provider network administration, management of flexible spending accounts, and other services.

Not only do clients gain from PSB's cost-effective oversight of each of these areas, but they reap the value of the firm's ties to a parent company that is an acknowledged expert in insurance and financial products.

Consider, for example, enrollment administration for benefit plans. PSB's in-house expertise covers every facet of benefits administration, including program design, automated employee enrollment via telephone and other media,

data input and confirmation, and post-enrollment reporting and analysis. (More than 500,000 separate enrollments were processed in 1994 alone.) PSB supports automated enrollments with a 45,000-square-foot warehouse dedicated to the storage, collation, and shipment of benefit packages and other communication materials—more than 4 million pieces annually. At the same time, The Prudential's PruNet database, as well as its many specialty benefit products, adds value to the enrollment process through the conduit of PSB.

Factors of Excellence

Two factors stand out in PSB's attainment of outsourcing excellence: technology and people. Though this may seem paradoxical—at many firms, the two are at odds—PSB is the kind of organization in which sophisticated people and technology support and enhance each other.

PSB employs the newest systems technology to outperform competitors in the fields of data collection, management, analysis, and reporting. Two leading components in PSB's information infrastructure are its voice response system (VRS) and optical character recognition (OCR).

VRS utilizes state-of-the-art software and fiber-optic technology to provide crucial telephone-based administrative services, such as inventory tracking and requisitions, bank loan inquiries, order entry, fee quotes, service schedules, marketing surveys, registrations at schools and universities, and customer service inquiries, as well as a variety of benefit program transactions. In fact, clients can choose to support their employee-retention operations with a turnkey VRS that will result in a comprehensive customer service network.

OCR is information processing technology that represents a quantum leap in quality and time efficiency over old-fashioned data entry. By "reading" documents at the rate of 3,000 per hour, OCR technology dramatically lowers costs and improves accuracy by a ratio of 4-to-1 over industry standards for manual input. PSB uses OCR for forms processing, survey tabulation, polling public opinions, mortgage and loan applications, mail-order processing, credit card billing, and other client services.

Of course, all this technology would be wasted without trained and motivated employees to properly apply it. PSB employs 850 people who are experts not only at

the requirements of their position, but also at dealing fairly and professionally with the organization's clients. Thanks to an extensive training program in customer sensitivity, quality control, and effective listening, PSB customer service representatives are particularly skilled in providing superior administrative services with a human face.

This commitment to excellence is given its most succinct form in The Prudential Core Values: Worthy of Trust, Customer Focused, Respect for Others, and Winning. Begun as the Prudential Friendly Society in 1875 and converted to a mutual company beginning in 1915, The Prudential's belief in a customer-first management philosophy has resulted in a rich and pluralistic corporate culture in which PSB proudly participates.

"The best companies know that focus is the secret of success," says Wadsworth. "PSB follows its own advice—we focus on our core mission of providing outstanding benefits outsourcing." By offering firms of many sizes the opportunity to improve their benefit programs while streamlining their costs, Prudential Service Bureau is proving to be a worthy addition to The Prudential's legacy.

TWO FACTORS STAND OUT IN PRUDENTIAL SERVICE BUREAU'S ATTAINMENT OF OUTSOURCING EXCELLENCE: TECHNOLOGY AND PEOPLE. PRUDENTIAL IS THE KIND OF ORGANIZATION IN WHICH SOPHISTICATED PEOPLE AND TECHNOLOGY SUPPORT AND ENHANCE EACH OTHER.

"LOUISVILLE IS GOOD FOR BUSINESS," SAYS MARK SELLERS, A VETERAN of the environmental consulting and design industry, and president of ADVENT. "From a progressive education system, to low crime and the quality of life that comes from a midsize city, to a pro-business culture in local government, Louisville's an ideal home for ADVENT." ◆ Since opening its Louisville office in 1992, ADVENT has become one

ADVENT ENVIRONMENTAL HAS PROSPERED UNDER THE LEADERSHIP OF VICE PRESIDENT LARRY DIETSCH (LEFT) AND PRESIDENT MARK SELLERS (RIGHT).

BY FOCUSING ON INDUSTRIAL CLIENT NEEDS ADVENT HAS BECOME ONE OF THE AREA'S PREMIER PROFESSIONAL ENGINEERING AND ENVIRONMENTAL CONSULTING FIRMS (BELOW).

of the area's premier professional engineering and environmental consulting firms, serving the top 10 percent of Fortune 500 companies in a variety of industries, including chemical distribution, synthetic organic chemical manufacturing, heavy manufacturing, and distilled spirits.

At the Forefront of Environmental Consulting

Complex regulations and a burgeoning sense of corporate responsibility have made environmental programs one of the top priorities for successful companies. ADVENT serves a growing number of these companies, helping them analyze risks, manage costs, and develop a strategy to contain and remedy contamination.

While ADVENT has found its niche in industrial consulting, its services go beyond environmental engineering issues. "We often must address the financial and regulatory aspects of these issues as well," says

Larry Dietsch, vice president and head of operations in Louisville. "We work closely with our clients' management team—including legal counsel, financial advisers, and technical staff—to bring our projects to a successful conclusion."

Through the application of a unique blend of resources in the engineering and scientific disciplines, ADVENT provides comprehensive environmental consulting and design services in the fields of industrial wastewater, hazardous wastes, regulatory compliance, and water resources.

The Human Factor in a Technical Field

"The key to doing the job right is individual service," says Dietsch. "Although it's a very technical field, there's a lot of one-on-one interaction with the client. In most cases, we function as an extension of their own environmental staff."

"We attend many of our clients' meetings and help them estab-

lish budgets. We try to design a cleanup plan that fits their goals," says Hugh Taylor, executive vice president and treasurer. "In a lot of industries, companies just don't have enough internal resources to keep up with all the regulations that may apply to them."

The importance of close interaction has led ADVENT to be selective about its clients. "We won't take on assignments if we don't feel there's the right kind of fit," says Dietsch.

ADVENT has attracted professionals who are not only highly experienced in environmental consulting, but also have in-depth experience in the industries they serve. "Most of our senior staff are registered professionals. Our clients are confident that their consultant truly understands their current needs and the trends affecting them," says Sellers.

Employing top professionals is also one of the firm's biggest challenges. "Our greatest assets walk out the door at the end of each day," Sellers explains. "We not only have to take care of our customer base, we also have to focus on taking good care of our employees. Many of our staff are senior personnel who came here from large firms that lost the employee focus. That's something we won't do."

Maintaining a Tight Focus

Sellers notes that because of an increasing awareness of environmental issues, there are thousands of environmental consulting firms in the United States. ADVENT has grown by remaining focused on its particular niche—industrial environmental compliance and corrective action issues.

This approach typically leads to long-term relationships with clients. "More than three-quarters of our work is repeat business," says Sellers. "That's where our future is. Sometimes we'll tell a client they don't need our help for a particular project because we want them to come back to us when we can really offer them something valuable."

While Sellers says many people aren't familiar with the company, he notes that in certain industries, ADVENT is "practically a household name." Many of ADVENT's projects are confidential in nature. "Not many companies publicize their problems or wish us to disclose that they are a client of ours," Sellers explains.

ADVENT has grown so rapidly, it has opened new regional offices at the rate of about one every other year, while revenues have grown about 40 percent per year. These figures are significant since the industry overall is declining by 5 percent or so a year. "We are indisputably the fastest-growing envi-

ronmental engineering firm in town," says Dietsch. ADVENT's goal is to continue the current growth pattern in a controlled manner while maintaining quality service delivery.

Firmly Attached to Louisville

ADVENT's employees in Louisville say they are delighted with the city for many reasons. According to Sellers, one of the reasons they chose to locate the firm in Louisville is a pro-business attitude among local government officials. He cited major local activities—such as airport expansion, downtown development along the riverfront, and recognition of the need to redevelop older industrial properties—as examples of the proactive political climate in the city. Plus, Louisville is located near many of the types of industries that make up ADVENT's client base.

Sellers, who sits on the board of the Kentucky Opera Association, says he strongly encourages all of

ADVENT's senior staff to become involved in local organizations, from business groups to the arts.

With the rapid advancements of technology, new contaminants produce new regulations—regulations that mean a continuing need for assistance to find the acceptable balance between efficient operations and environmental responsibility. ADVENT will be there to help.

OF ADVENT's TOP PROFESSIONALS, SAYS COMPANY PRESIDENT MARK SELLERS, "OUR GREATEST ASSETS WALK OUT THE DOOR AT THE END OF EACH DAY." ADVENT PERSONNEL FUNCTION AS AN EXTENSION OF THE CLIENT'S ENVIRONMENTAL STAFF.

© DAN DRY / DAN DRY & ASSOCIATES

© DAN DRY / DAN DRY & ASSOCIATES

COLUMBIA/HCA HEALTHCARE CORPORATION

THE HEALTH CARE INDUSTRY IS IN A CONSTANT STATE OF change, with new regulations forcing health care organizations to alter the way they do business. While some will fail to adapt and eventually close, Columbia/HCA Healthcare Corporation—the largest health care provider in the world—is leading the way by adapting and growing to offer superior, uncompromised services in streamlined and more efficient ways.

Positioned to be one of the top health care providers of the 21st century, Columbia/HCA owns more beds than any other hospital corporation in Kentucky and, in fact, the world. The Kentucky Division employs approximately 11,000 people and serves a complete range of health care needs, from inpatient/outpatient care to rehabilitation and skilled nursing services.

Growth through Acquisition

Columbia/HCA's success was no accident. Its growth is part of a purposeful plan that President and Chief Executive Officer Richard L. Scott created in 1987. From its origins as Columbia Healthcare in Texas, the company embarked on a path that would lead it to successfully complete three of the largest corporate mergers in the health care industry.

First, Columbia merged with Galen Health Care, Inc. of Louisville in 1993. Galen had been created when Humana Inc. split into separate companies. Then, in February of 1994, Columbia merged with HCA (Hospital Corporation of America).

"HCA's portfolio of hospitals was strong, and we have realized significant efficiencies in markets where both Columbia and HCA operated," says Jim Pickle, president of the Columbia/HCA Kentucky Division. "In other markets, growth opportunities exist through Columbia's strategy of adding services to create comprehensive networks."

A third merger—with HealthTrust, Inc., completed in April 1995—made Columbia the 10th-largest employer in the United States, with 190,000 employees. The company currently operates 320 hospitals and more than 100 outpatient surgery centers in 36 states, England, and Switzerland.

A Strategically Important Market

Columbia/HCA owns and operates three Louisville hospitals—

Audubon Regional Medical Center, Suburban Medical Center, and Southwest Hospital—totaling more than 1,000 beds and employing approximately 4,500 people. Additionally, Columbia/HCA owns a variety of home health agencies and is the largest provider of home health care services in the state.

"Kentucky—Louisville in particular—is a very important market for us," Pickle says. "In fact, two of our Louisville hospitals are among the largest in the company, and we are a major economic presence here."

Outstanding Facilities

Columbia stands out from the other hospital providers in both Louisville and the other areas it serves. "It's our network approach to providing health care, our aggressive growth philosophy and the quality of our facilities," says Pickle. "We offer a full range of health care services in very defined areas and we measure the quality of those services. Two of our Louisville hospitals recently received Accreditation with Commendation from the Joint Commission of Accreditation of Healthcare Organizations, which is the highest distinction bestowed by the Joint Commission. The third, Audubon Regional Medical Center, will be surveyed next year. We also take patient satisfaction very seriously. The Gallup Organization surveys a sample of all inpatients every month. Sixty-four percent of patients in our Louisville facilities are 'very satisfied' with their overall stay as compared to 48 percent of patients in the non-Columbia hospitals."

Evidence of this is clear in the Louisville market's outstanding facilities, such as Audubon Regional Medical Center, home of the Audubon Heart Institute and the Neuroscience Center of Excellence; Suburban Medical Center, with its high-tech laser surgery center and its Advanced Orthopedic Center;

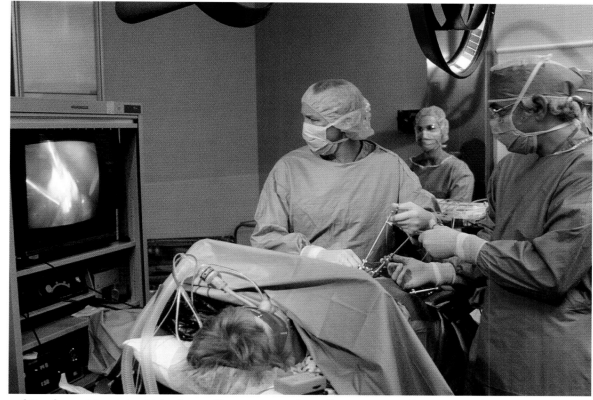

and Southwest Hospital, which offers a range of specialized diagnostic, surgical, and emergency services.

The Lipid Center at Audubon Regional Medical Center is a particularly outstanding example. It was established in 1986 as a clinic specializing in the prevention of cardiovascular disease through the detection of cholesterol disorders. The Lipid Center's hospital laboratory is fully accredited by the Federal Centers for Disease Control.

The only facility of its kind in Kentucky, the Lipid Center is now an active research site in areas such as atherosclerosis, heart failure, hypertension, and diabetes mellitus. And, scientific publications from the Lipid Center have appeared in highly respected health care publications such as the *New England Journal of Medicine* and the *Journal of the Kentucky Medical Association.*

Another Columbia service that is unique to the area is the Wound Care Center at Suburban. The center specializes in the treatment of chronic, nonhealing wounds, which

affect an estimated 3 million to 5 million people in the United States. Wounds treated at the center are often associated with inadequate blood flow and occur often among diabetics.

The Columbia Wound Care Center offers leading-edge treatment programs including those that integrate Procuren or Growth Factor Therapy. This therapy uses a patient's own blood to promote the healing of a chronic wound. With these advanced treatments available, there is hope for many patients who are suffering from nonhealing wounds.

A Force for Dynamic Change

It's obvious that the people of Columbia/HCA are a dynamic force changing the health care industry from within. While Congress and the states debate the elements of various health care reform plans, the people and physicians associated with Columbia/HCA will continue to lead the way by developing solutions that will not only simplify hospital operations, but also improve quality.

SURGEONS AT SUBURBAN MEDICAL CENTER ARE TEAMING UP WITH THE LATEST TECHNOLOGY SO THAT MANY SURGICAL PROCEDURES CAN NOW BE PERFORMED ON AN OUTPATIENT BASIS (ABOVE).

W**HAT'S IT TAKE TO BE THE BEST? FIFTH THIRD BANK SEEMS** to have a good handle on the question. Since its founding more than 100 years ago, the bank's reputation for excellence has been affirmed again and again by almost every major voice in the industry. The publication *U.S. Banker* named Fifth Third the number one bank in the nation in 1995, the second time in

three years it earned the magazine's top rating. Likewise Salomon Brothers, in its 1994 Bank Annual Review, ranked Fifth Third the top-performing bank in the country, and that year Moody's placed the bank's dividend yield in the top 1 percent of all publicly traded companies—noting the bank increased its dividend more than 25 times in 20 years.

While accolades from high places are nice, the company knows whose opinion really counts—the customer's. Meeting the customer's needs day in and day out takes an ability to listen and a penchant for hard work. At Fifth Third, innovation and sound management are combined with the one value people never forget—good service. And that's why the organization is successful. No special program. No magic formula. The bank's slogan says it all: Working Hard to Be the Only Bank You'll Ever Need.

"In the service business, you have to constantly hustle," says James R. Gaunt, Fifth Third Bank

of Kentucky, Louisville, president and CEO. "You've got to work harder than the next guy."

New Avenues in Banking

Fifth Third's innovation and commitment are seen through the delivery of its services. In addition to traditional banking centers that make personal service number one, Fifth Third offers Bank Mart locations in select Kroger stores that provide the full range of banking services seven days a week, giving new meaning to the term banker's hours—in fact, transforming banker's hours into customer hours.

And with Jeanie Telephone Banking, many important features are just a phone call away. Jeanie customers can check balances, transfer funds, pay bills, and verify paid checks or other transactions by using a Touch-Tone phone. The Jeanie system includes automated teller machines in every part of the community and point-of-sale locations that allow customers to purchase at the checkout counter using a Jeanie Card.

"The trend over the next 10 years is definitely toward more automation and less bricks and mortar," says Gaunt. "We're looking toward a new generation of services that will be delivered directly to the customers—and always with the same level of service that has brought us to where we are today."

Working Hard to Be the Only Bank You'll Ever Need

Fifth Third strives to meet virtually any banking or financial need that a consumer may have. From students to senior citizens, the bank tailors its checking and savings vehicles to meet the individual situation. Its Club 53 Account for folks 50 and older brings an unparalleled level of discounts and premiums. Likewise Fifth Third's family of One Accounts, in addition to great checking services, entitles clients to substantial discounts on other bank products, such as mortgages and installment loans. A variety of credit cards are also offered.

In the area of trust and investments, Fifth Third provides expert asset management for both personal estates and organizational needs. Fifth Third's Fountain Square family of mutual funds has a history of

FIFTH THIRD BANK IS A PARTNER IN THE GROWTH AND DEVELOPMENT OF LOUISVILLE BUSINESSES SUCH AS GREEN BULL, INC., MAKERS OF COMMERCIAL AND INDUSTRIAL LADDER PRODUCTS (BELOW). FIFTH THIRD VICE PRESIDENT BILL OTTEN (CENTER LEFT) AND SENIOR VICE PRESIDENT ROBERT EVERSOLE (CENTER RIGHT) MEET WITH GREEN BULL INC.'S PRESIDENT JOHN BECKER (LEFT) AND CONTROLLER CHRIS PRENTICE.

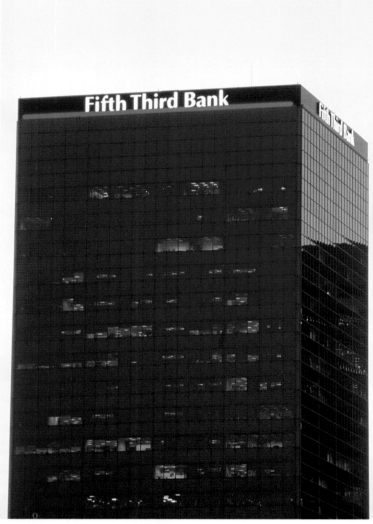

of flexible financing options for a broad range of clients—from small proprietorships to Fortune 1000 companies.

Fifth Third provides processing for electronic funds and point-of-sale activities through its subsidiary, Midwest Payment Systems (MPS), which handles Visa and

MasterCard transactions for more than 14,000 retail outlets. MPS also has agreements with Master-Card international to handle processing of its debit cards and to provide MasterCard point-of-service capabilities through the Jeanie network. The agreement allows cardholders to use the Jeanie card at more than 12 million MasterCard merchant locations worldwide.

A Community Spirit

From orchestras to libraries, crusades to festivals, Fifth Third is a leading supporter of the activities that enrich the community for everyone. The bank also teams up with a variety of not-for-profit groups and government agencies to make its financial resources, such as mortgages and business loans, more available to wider segments of the community.

Fifth Third believes that a united community is a stronger community, and the bank is committed to being part of the Louisville-area's growth and well-being.

"Louisville has a diverse economy and a growing economic base," says Gaunt, noting that Louisville has the fundamental things that businesses need, including affordable real estate and a good transportation system. "We think Louisville is a great community," says Gaunt, "and a great community deserves a great bank."

At Fifth Third Bank, innovation and sound management are combined with the one value people never forget—good service. The bank's slogan says it all: Working Hard to Be the Only Bank You'll Ever Need.

cracking the top rankings. The bank also offers retirement products, such as the Fountain Square 401(k) Advantage, which features a voice-response telephone system as well as employee education programs. Not-for-profit organizations enjoy the Fountain Square 403(b) program, and Fifth Third has a team dedicated to foundation and charitable funds management. Through its subsidiary, Fifth Third Securities, Inc., the bank offers brokerage and related services through any of

the bank's conveniently located banking centers.

Commercial Activity

In addition to retail banking, Fifth Third places heavy emphasis on the commercial side. Commercial checking and savings vehicles, data processing, leasing services, brokerage, and an award-winning International Department headline the bank's strengths in this area. In 1994 the bank's international team was awarded the President's E Award from the U.S. Department of Commerce, recognizing mastery of "exports, excellence, expansion, and effort," as stated by the Kentucky World Trade Conference.

Fifth Third is also an industry leader in treasury management services and the bank offers a variety

THE MIND-BOGGLING ARRAY OF INSURANCE PRODUCTS AVAILABLE to today's consumers can confuse just about anybody. This is especially true of individual buyers, who may not have the experience of a group benefits manager in evaluating competing products. That's why Acordia Personal was created—to provide individuals with a single source for every insurance need. The Louisville company offers a wide

variety of quality, affordable benefits to individuals throughout Kentucky, with caring customer service to back it up.

One-Stop Shopping, One Customer at a Time

Acordia Personal is a full-service insurance brokerage offering a wide range of benefits, including medical, dental, life, and disability coverage, as well as annuities and other investment vehicles. Acordia also provides a variety of administrative services such as enrollment, billing, and claims processing.

Acordia Personal offers insurance products from leading carriers around the nation. In fact, a full-time commitment to service is the source of the company's success. Thanks to Acordia Personal, individuals can enjoy the same one-stop shopping for benefits that leading brokerages, like parent company Acordia, offer American businesses.

Helping Seniors Bridge the Gap

Seniors are an important part of the individual health benefits market. For example, retirees relying on Medicare to cover health care costs often find they need additional coverage of items and services for which Medicare does not pay, such as deductibles, coinsurance, and prescription drugs. Option 2000 Medicare Supplement, offered by an affiliate of Anthem Blue Cross and Blue Shield, is marketed exclusively by Acordia Personal and can help fill the gaps. Option 2000 Medicare Supplement is offered by Southeastern United Medigroup, Inc., an affiliate of Anthem Blue

Cross and Blue Shield, independent licensees of the Blue Cross and Blue Shield Association.

Leader in Long-Term Care

Another area of concern to the elderly is long-term care. Though the cost of nursing home care averages $30,000 a year, neither Medicare nor most Medicare supplement policies offer much in the way of long-term care. However, Acordia Personal offers a long-term care plan that provides quality care in the member's home, eliminating the need for an expensive nursing home stay.

National Commitment to Local Service

Acordia Personal is part of Indianapolis-based Acordia, which oversees a nationwide network of brokerage, managed care, and consulting companies. Founded in 1989 by The Associated Group, Acordia became the nation's seventh-largest insurance brokerage in only five years.

Despite this growth, Acordia remains committed to a corporate strategy of locally controlled subsid-

iaries. By developing strong ties to their communities, companies like Acordia Personal learn how to better serve the insurance and financial needs of customers on a permanent basis. The local touch is a big plus in providing customer service. When a member needs help, the company's representatives aren't half a continent away, and Acordia Personal consultants often visit members in person.

Acordia Personal offers products that combine the best innovations in coverage and quality with an old-fashioned commitment to the people who depend on them.

CLOCKWISE FROM RIGHT: BOTH INDIVIDUALS AND FAMILIES CAN ENJOY A WIDE RANGE OF BENEFITS AVAILABLE THROUGH ACORDIA PERSONAL.

SENIORS WILL FIND COMPLETE INDIVIDUAL COVERAGE AND EXCELLENT LONG-TERM CARE PLANS WITH ACORDIA PERSONAL.

ACORDIA PERSONAL PRESIDENT AND CHIEF EXECUTIVE OFFICER JUDE THOMPSON GUIDES A COMPANY OFFERING A WIDE VARIETY OF QUALITY, AFFORDABLE BENEFITS TO INDIVIDUALS THROUGHOUT KENTUCKY, WITH CARING CUSTOMER SERVICE TO BACK IT UP.

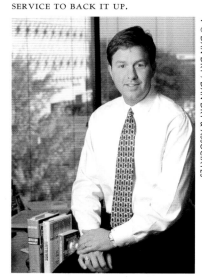

PHOTOGRAPHERS

Paul R. Bayens, a native of Louisville, is a retired photographer specializing in flowers in scenic landscapes. Formerly he worked as a sports reporter for a small weekly newspaper, contributing some of his photos to the publication. Bayens' favorite subjects are landscapes and wildlife as well as landmarks, and he is an admitted sports fanatic, participating in track and field in the Senior Olympics since 1987.

Timothy Bickel, a native of Indianapolis, works for Eastman Kodak Company. Bickel specializes in wedding photos, portraiture, and stock photography.

Jim Bryan, originally from Boston, attended the University of Louisville, where he obtained a B.S. in finance and economics, and an M.B.A. with an emphasis in marketing. He is the president of Braine Enterprises, specializing in music composition and publishing. Bryan's photography has earned awards in such categories as floral, nature, reflections, windows, and the world of water, and he enjoys creating slide presentations, combining his own ethereal photographs with the New Age music he has composed.

William N. Clark, a Louisville native, has seen his work published in *Trains* magazine and *The Dixie Line*, a Louisville and Nashville Railroad Historical Society publication. Specializing in railroad and landscape photography, Clark counts historic transportation equipment, cityscapes, and seascapes among his favorite subjects. He is a graduate of the University of Louisville with a degree in physics.

Zeljko Cvijanovic, a native of Yugoslavia, moved to the Louisville area in 1991. The owner of Zeljko Cvijanovic Photography, Cvijanovic previously worked as a photographer on cruise ships before settling in Louisville. His work can be seen in numerous publications, including *Inside Louisville, Kentucky Derby*

Magazine, and *Derby Fever*. He has also created promotional and corporate advertising campaigns for such organizations as Chi Chi's Inc., Coldwell Banker, Gorden Hundley Builders, Re/Max Properties East, and The Prudential.

Gretchen Davis, who was born in Michigan, moved to Louisville in 1994. Having studied at Indiana University, University College in London, and the School of the Art Institute of Chicago, Davis is employed by Dan Dry & Associates. Davis has had photographs published in *Cincinnati* magazine and *Photographers Market*, and is a coeditor and writer for *Image*, an American Society of Magazine Photographers publication for the Ohio Valley. Davis has traveled extensively and enjoys mountain biking, hiking, running, and gourmet cooking. She is currently building a darkroom in her home for black-and-white film processing.

David A. English, who originates from Brandenburg, Kentucky, moved to Louisville in 1979. Specializing in commercial photography, he works for Warren Lynch & Associates. English enjoys shooting tabletop photography and working on large-scale projects, such as sporting goods brochures. English has won a Louisville Graphic Design Association (LGDA) award, a Louie award, and an Addy award.

Charlene Faris, a native of Fleming County, Kentucky, is the owner and operator of Charlene Faris Photos and the director of an exhibition group called Photography: A Diverse Focus. Specializing in travel, historic, and inspirational photography, Faris has won numerous awards during her career as a photographer, including several honors from the National League of American Pen Women art shows. She was a 1994 Pulitzer Prize nominee for wedding photos of Lyle Lovett and Julia Roberts, which have now been published in 25 different nations. Faris is a graduate of Ball State University.

Larry Foster, a native of Illinois, moved to the Louisville area in 1973. A self-employed painter, his areas of photographic specialty include nature and people. Foster is a two-time winner of the *Courier-Journal* Scene Contest magazine photo contest, and he has achieved two first-prize awards in the categories of landscape and close-up photography for the Scene Photo Scenic Weekend contest. Two of Foster's photographs can be seen in the Louisville Zoo calendar, and he has donated his photographic services to the American Cancer Society, the Humane Society, and public television. Foster has attended Jefferson Community College and the University of Louisville.

Jeanne Freibert, owner of Jeanne Freibert Studio, is a native Louisvillian. A magna cum laude graduate from Murray State University, she specializes in editorial, commercial, and corporate photography. Freibert's work can be seen in such publications as the *Courier-Journal, Louisville* magazine, and *Choices* magazine, and previous clients include Fairchild Publications, WHAS TV, Ashland Oil, Ford Motor Company, and the Times-Journal Company. Among numerous other honors, Freibert won the silver award at the 1995 LGDA 100 Show.

Jeff Gardner, a lifelong Louisvillian, attended the University of Louisville and Jefferson Community College, where he received an associate degree in photography. Winner of a Louie and an LGDA award, he currently works for Warren Lynch & Associates, specializing in commercial photography. Gardner enjoys whitewater sports, farming, raising beef cattle, and being with his children, Dustin and Jesse, and his wife, Hsiao-Ling.

Stephen E. Gilman, a native of Louisville, moved to Boston in 1993 where he currently works for the New England Medical Center as a research administrator. A professional documentary photographer until his move to Boston, Gilman has traveled extensively, documenting life in such far-

away places as Israel and Guatemala. Gilman has studied at the Harvard School of Public Health, Hebrew University of Jerusalem in Israel, and University of Salamanca in Spain.

Kenneth Hayden, owner and operator of Kenneth Hayden Photography, is a native of Owensboro, Kentucky. Specializing in editorial illustration, portraiture, and photography for corporate communications, Hayden has worked for DuPont, IBM, Crown Publishers, Harmony House Publishers, Sotheby's, Christie's, Geo, *Der Speigel, Time,* and *Newsweek.* Hayden received his degree in photography from Brescia College in Owensboro and continues to take classes in painting, drawing, and printmaking at both Brescia and the University of Louisville.

Gertrude Hudson, originally from Washington County, Kentucky, moved to Louisville in 1952. Although she has no formal training in photography, Hudson loves to take pictures, especially nature shots. She also enjoys traveling, both in the United States and overseas.

Dan Kremer, born in Evansville, Indiana, is employed by Warren Lynch & Associates. He has earned an associate degree in commercial and industrial photography and has received a Louie award. Kremer has also been published in *Communication Arts.*

Susan Lustig, who moved to the Louisville area in 1984, has a bachelor of science degree in wildlife biology from Colorado State University. The owner of Susan Lustig Photography, specializing in equestrian and Thoroughbred racing photography, she has been published in *The Texas Thoroughbred, The Blood Horse, Thoroughbred Times, The Backstretch Magazine,* and *Spur.* In addition to photographing horses, Lustig shows horses across the country.

Linda Morton, a native of Louisville, entered photography from a business background three years ago.

An officer of the Louisville Photographic Society, Morton competes regionally and has won several local awards. She has begun work on an exhibit with the Frankfort Arts Foundation and is launching publication of her stock photography in *Louisville: A River Serenade*. Morton works in photographic art sales, as a studio assistant for a national magazine, and as a freelance writer. People, architecture, and nature are her favorite subjects.

John Nation, originally from Owensboro, Kentucky, moved to Louisville in 1977. A self-employed photographer, Nation's primary client is *Louisville* magazine, where he does editorial and location shooting. Nation received a degree in drawing and painting from the University of Louisville and attended the U.S. Naval School of Photography.

Jeff Offutt, a lifelong Louisville resident, enjoys photographing people, crowds, and unusual images he encounters along the streets of the city.

Lynn T. Shea moved to Louisville from Frankfort more than 30 years ago. Shea minored in art at Centre College; studied at Kentucky State University, Spalding College, and Bellarmine College; and is currently enrolled at the University of Louisville. An amateur photographer, Shea has won many awards, both nationally and internationally, and she has been published in both the *Lee Almanac* and the *Best of Photography Annual* for several different years. Shea loves to travel, having visited some 50 countries and having lived in Europe for a time, but art and art collecting are her primary interests.

Ralph H. Sidway moved to the Louisville area from Buffalo in 1972. A graduate of Transylvania University, he works at Murphy's Camera in Louisville. Sidway specializes in black-and-white fine-art photography and has won numerous awards for his work, including the 1993 Decatur Arts Festival Purchase Award and the

1995 Ohio Valley annual photography award. In addition to fine-art photography, Sidway shoots stock photography and does commercial freelance work. Furthermore, he is an accomplished singer-songwriter.

Donald J. Sivori, a Louisville native, is a self-taught photographer who works for Commercial, Inc. Specializing in landscape photography, especially during dawn and dusk, Sivori is a four-time winner in the *Courier-Journal* Scene Contest. Sivori occasionally photographs wildlife and sports.

Ethel B. Stoke, a graduate of Brevard Junior College and the University of Louisville, is a Louisville native. Her work can be seen in the Louisville Zoo calendar, in the Louisville tourism guide, and in several newsletters. Stoke was awarded first prize in the black-and-white photography category in the *Courier-Journal* Scene Contest and in the Northern Tissue national contest, and she has won numerous ribbons at the Kentucky state fair. She has been a member of the Louisville Photographic Society since 1978 and she loves

photographing children. Stoke and her husband travel extensively.

Beverly Ann Tully is a freelance photographer from New Albany, Indiana. A graduate of Indiana University Southeast, Tully is a retired newspaper photojournalist and a member of the Louisville Photographic Society. Her photographs have been published in several magazines.

William F. Van Hook specializes in stock photography, focusing on children, animals, and landscapes as his subjects. Originally from Fairland, Indiana, he attended Indiana University Southeast and currently works for Photography Like Magic. Van Hook won the James H. Rowden poetry award and has been published in the St. Matthew's 45th anniversary booklet, the *Louisville Music News*, and the *Jeffersonville Evening News*. He enjoys experimenting with light in his photography.

INDEX OF SPONSORS

▲▼ JEANNE FREIBERT

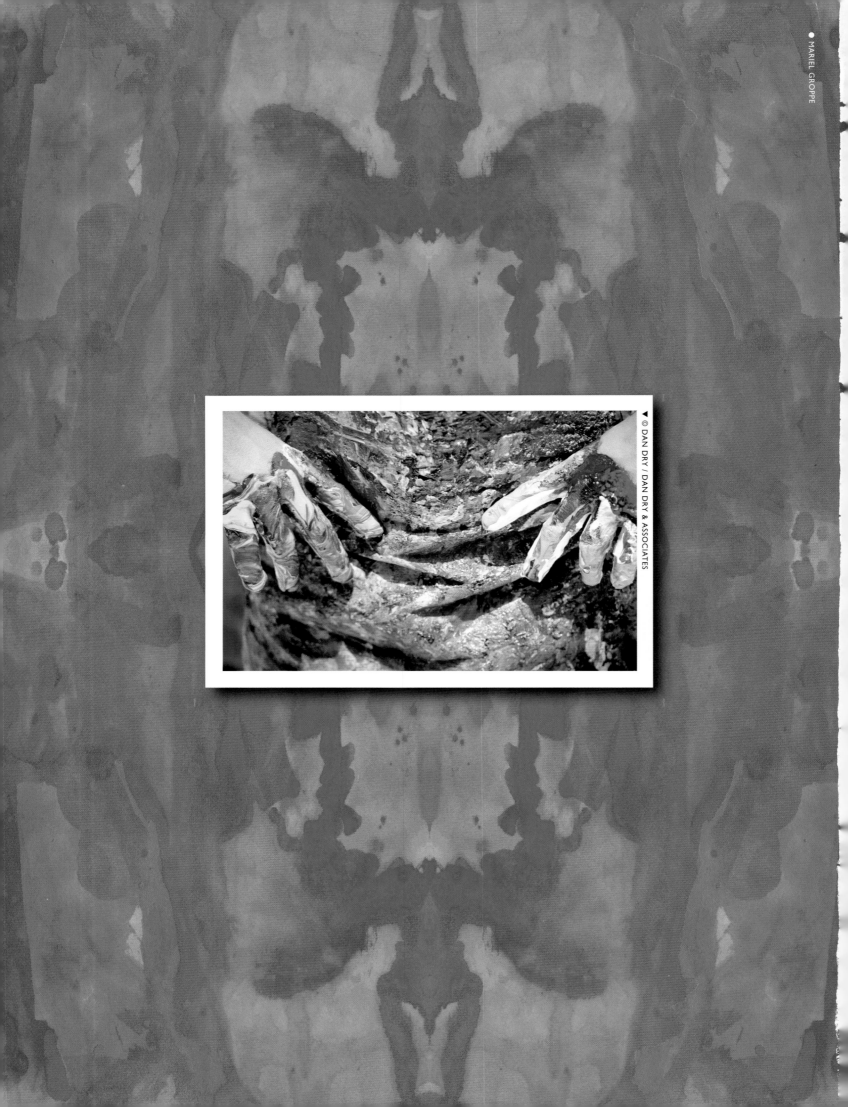